THREE PLAYS BY UGO BETTI

THREE PLAYS BY
UGO BETTI

THE QUEEN AND THE REBELS
THE BURNT FLOWER-BED
SUMMERTIME

translated,
and with a Foreword, by
HENRY REED

GROVE PRESS, INC. NEW YORK

Library of Congress Catalog Card Number: 58-5442

Second Printing 1959

Three Plays by Ugo Betti is published in three editions:
An Evergreen Book (E-90)
A hard bound edition
A specially bound, Limited Edition of 100 numbered copies

Grove Press Books and Evergreen Books
are published by Barney Rosset at Grove Press, Inc.
64 University Place, New York 3, N. Y.

MANUFACTURED IN THE UNITED STATES OF AMERICA

FOREWORD

Ugo Betti was born on February the 4th 1892 at Camerino, in the Italian Marches, in a street which is now named after him. He was the son of a doctor who in 1900 moved to Parma, to take up the directorship of the hospital in that city. Here Betti was educated in classics. A brief biographical note in a recent edition of his three posthumous plays says that his early youth was mainly devoted to sport. Maybe; but he somehow found time to translate Catullus's "Marriage of Thetis and Peleus", which was published in Camerino in 1910, when he was still only eighteen. He graduated in law at Parma, but his career was interrupted by the first world war. He was commissioned in the artillery, was decorated, and in 1917 was taken prisoner and sent to Germany. Here he began to write the verses which were to be included in 1922 in his first volume of original work, *The Thoughtful King*. He resumed his practice of law at Parma after the war, eventually becoming a *pretore* and later a judge. In 1930 he was moved to Rome, where until a few years before his death he was a magistrate in the High Court. He died on June the 9th 1953.

During his later years Betti had become accepted as the leading dramatist in Italy in the generation that followed Pirandello. It is probable that most critics in Italy to-day regard him as a greater dramatic artist than Pirandello. This is not to disparage Pirandello, the splendour of whose finest theatrical work is not in doubt. Nevertheless I think that the view is a right one which sees Pirandello's best achievement in his brilliant and voluminous prose fiction. It is quite otherwise with Betti. Pirandello worked his way into the drama by dramatising his own short stories. But Betti's dedication to the drama began early enough for us to assume that it was his original and main intention. His three volumes of lyric poetry, his three collections of short stories, and his single short novel have a distinction of their own; but they can fairly be regarded as the marginalia to the succession of twenty-five dramatic works which they accompanied, and whose thought and preoccupation they echo, underline and occasionally anticipate.

It may be of use to English readers to have some brief non-critical account of Betti's progress through his quarter-century of playwriting. Apart from a handful of comedies, his plays are tragic in cast, and often violent, frightening or bizarre. They are also—increasingly so in the later plays—austerely Christian in implication. His subject is wickedness; perhaps his life as a judge showed him more curious varieties of it than most of us come upon; at all events he studies its preposterous growths with an habituated candour. His first play, *La Padrona*, written in 1926, was awarded the first prize in a dramatic competition in Rome. It is a short three-act play, harsh, concentrated and astonishingly competent technically; its subject, put baldly, is the contest between Marina, representing life, and Anna, representing death, for the anguished, dilapidated soul of Pietro; Marina is his second wife, Anna his daughter by his first marriage. Life does in fact win the contest, but one has no sense of a happy ending. In it, Betti seems to have deliberately set himself the task of not giving in to the side of himself expressed in his early fairy-tale lyrics. He makes similar self-corrective gestures elsewhere in the course of his work. Here the result is as if Maeterlinck had been disciplined to the manner of Verga.

In only a few of Betti's plays is precise locality indicated. The scene of *La Padrona* is simply a "poor home". In the plays that immediately follow there is a sense of Northern Europe, though the characters in general have Italian names. The sudden fusing of this remote atmospheric feeling with Betti's own intimate knowledge of the courts of justice precipitates his first masterpiece, *Landslide at the North Station* (1932) where an investigation into the responsibility for an industrial disaster is found gradually to involve a whole society. It is in this play that one of Betti's major themes emerges: man's wish for judgment upon his actions. It was this play—the fifth of Betti's plays to be staged—that first persuaded a large body of critics that a considerable dramatic talent had appeared and could no longer be ignored; it could, however, still be called "literary", and was: the word being pejorative in intent. It was perhaps a determination to show that his methods and manner were a choice and not an involuntary eccentric compulsion—and perhaps also a simple wish for commercial success—that persuaded Betti to write the comedies that occupied him during the late 'thirties. It is to this group that *Land of Holidays* (known to the English stage as *Summertime*, and included in this volume) belongs. This at least won public favour, and Betti presumably felt that, his point made, he might return to his own interests.

FOREWORD

The series of thirteen plays which Betti produced between 1941 and his death in 1953 must be among the greatest creative outbursts in dramatic literature. In none of these is there what we are used to in England as "religious drama"; yet they are all concerned with one aspect or another of men's fatal disregard or defiance of God. *The Queen and the Rebels* and *The Burnt Flower-bed* come towards the end of the group. They are the only plays dealing with political material in the whole of Betti's work; and the essential theme is scarcely political, even in these. Most of the other plays are concerned with the more desperate relationships of man and woman. I have no wish to pre-judge them for audiences to whom they are not yet available; but there may be no harm in suggesting that they confront us with a dramatist whose unusual maturity of vision gives us pity and terror, where we normally find only their modern substitutes, pathos and hysteria. In a play such as *Crime on Goat Island*, where passionate sexual feeling is at its densest and most degraded, there is still a sense of classical tragedy. It is not simply a question of dramatic structure. The sense persists in plays like *The Gambler*, *Woman in Flight*, and *Irene Innocente*, where the structure is far from being classical.

. . . . .

These translations were originally commissioned by the Third Programme of the B.B.C., and produced by Mr. Donald MacWhinnie. They were considerably revised for their stage productions, and have been further revised for publication.

H. R.

CONTENTS

THE QUEEN AND THE REBELS

(*La Regina e gli Insorti*)

A Play in Four Acts

(1949)

CHARACTERS

Argia
Elisabetta
Amos
Biante
Raim
The Porter
Maupa
An Engineer
A Peasant
A Peasant-woman

And a number of travellers, soldiers and peasants, who do not speak.

The time is the present day.

THE QUEEN AND THE REBELS was performed at the Haymarket Theatre, London, on October 26th, 1955, with the following cast:

ARGIA	IRENE WORTH
ELISABETTA	GWENDOLINE WATFORD
AMOS	LEO MCKERN
BIANTE	ALAN TILVERN
RAIM	DUNCAN LAMONT
THE PORTER	JOHN KIDD
MAUPA	BRIAN WALLACE
AN ENGINEER	JOHN GILL
A PEASANT	PATRICK MAGEE
A PEASANT-WOMAN	MARY LLEWELLIN
A YOUNG PEASANT	ANGELA LLOYD

Travellers, Peasants, Soldiers: John Herrington, John Nettleton, Gordon Richardson, Jack Good, John Ronane, Kevin O'Keeffe, Kenneth Toye, Joe Goodman, Patricia Kneale.

The Play was produced by Frank Hauser

The Scenery was designed by Audrey Cruddas

The Play was presented by Henry Sherek

ACT ONE

The scene, which is the same throughout the play, represents a large hall in the main public building in a hill-side village. There are signs of disorder and neglect.

The stage is empty when the curtain rises. The time is sunset. After a moment the HALL-PORTER *comes in. He is humble and apologetic in manner.*

THE PORTER: (*to someone behind him*) Will you come this way, please?

A group of men and women come silently into the room. They are all carrying travelling-bags and cases.

THE PORTER: You can all wait in here for the time being.

ONE OF THE TRAVELLERS: (*cautiously*) We could wait just as well outside.

THE PORTER: Yes, but you can sit down in here. You'll find everything you want. This used to be the town-hall.

THE TRAVELLER: But we don't want to sit down. We want to get on. We're several hours late as it is.

THE PORTER: I'm sorry, sir. But you'll be all right in here. There are plenty of rooms, even if you have to stay the night.

THE TRAVELLER: Well, let's hope we don't have to stay the night! They told us we'd only be here half-an-hour, while the engine was cooling down.

THE PORTER: Yes, it's a stiff climb up here. The roads up those hills are very steep.

THE TRAVELLER: This is the third time they've stopped us to look at our papers. (*After a pause*) I'm a district engineer. I . . . (*dropping his voice*) Do you think they've some special reason for stopping us?

THE PORTER: No, no. They'll let you go on directly.

THE ENGINEER: Yes, but what are we waiting for?

THE PORTER: Sir, I . . . I really don't know what to say. I'm only the hall-porter here. That's to say, I *was* the hall-porter. Since the trouble began, I've been alone here. I have to look after everything. Anyway, will you all make yourselves comfortable?

THE ENGINEER: Is it possible to telegraph from here? Or telephone?

THE PORTER: All the lines are down. We're cut off from the world. And we're very out of the way here, in any case. I'll go and see if I can find you some blankets. (*A pause.*)

THE ENGINEER: Look here: I can only speak for myself, of course, but I dare say these other ladies and gentlemen feel much the same as I do about this. You surely realise that nobody's going to travel about just now unless they have to. Every one of us here has some important business or other to attend to. We've all been given permits to travel. Otherwise we wouldn't have come up here at a time like this. We aren't political people; we're just ordinary peaceful travellers. We've all had to pay very large sums of money for a wretched little seat in that lorry out there. And we've all had to get permission from——

THE PORTER: (*clearly unconvinced by his own words*) But you'll see, sir: they'll let you go on directly. (*A pause.*)

THE ENGINEER: Do you know who's in charge here?

THE PORTER: *I* don't, no, sir. I just take orders from everybody else.

THE ENGINEER: Is there anybody we can speak to?

THE PORTER: The trouble is they keep coming and going the whole time. They say there's a general expected here this evening; and a commissar.

THE ENGINEER: Then there's no one here now that we can speak to?

THE PORTER: The N.C.O.s are a bit rough-spoken, sir. The only one would be the interpreter. But no one takes much notice of him either, I'm afraid.

THE ENGINEER: Interpreter? What do they need an interpreter for?

THE PORTER: Oh, he's just an interpreter. He's an educated young man.

THE ENGINEER: Very well, then: fetch the interpreter.

THE PORTER: I'll get him, sir.

He goes out. The travellers sit down silently, here and there.

THE ENGINEER: I don't suppose it's anything to worry about. I saw some other people outside. They'd been held up too. It's obviously only another examination because we're so near the frontier. My own papers are all in order. But if there *is* anyone here who's . . . travelling irregularly . . . It might perhaps be as well if they had the courage to speak up straight away, and say so; before they get us all into trouble.

ANOTHER TRAVELLER: (*as though speaking to himself*) The large number of spies about the place doesn't exactly inspire people with much desire to "speak up", as you call it. In any case, it's obvious no one here is travelling irregularly. That would have been a little too simple-minded; or so I should have thought?

THE ENGINEER: Well, if that's the case, we ought to be on our way again in half-an-hour or so.

THE TRAVELLER: I can't say I share your optimism. It's been rather an odd journey, all along. Why did they make us come round this way in the first place? This village wasn't on our route at all. And the engine didn't need to cool down either. And why do we have all these inspections anyway? The only reasonable explanation is that they're looking for someone.

THE ENGINEER: One of us?

THE TRAVELLER: Though it's just as likely that they're simply being stupid and awkward, as usual. That's about all nine-tenths of the revolution comes to.

THE ENGINEER: I . . . think we'd better change the subject, if you don't mind. There's no point in . . .

THE TRAVELLER: In what?

THE ENGINEER: Well, after all, this upheaval has very great possibilities, when all's said and done.

THE TRAVELLER: You really think so?

THE ENGINEER: Yes. Yes, I do. Quite sincerely.

THE TRAVELLER: Couldn't you . . . spare yourself this extreme cautiousness? It looks rather as if the extremists aren't doing too well at the moment. You didn't notice, as we came along the road?

THE ENGINEER: Notice what?

THE TRAVELLER: Over towards the mountains. That faint crackling sound every now and then.

THE ENGINEER: What was it?

THE TRAVELLER: Rifle-fire. They're fighting near

here, on the far slope. Everything's hanging by a thread at the moment. It's possible the Unitary Government won't last the week out.

THE ENGINEER: A week. It doesn't take a week to shoot anybody. (*He drops his voice.*) I didn't notice the noises; I was too busy noticing the smell. Did you . . . catch that smell every now and then?

THE TRAVELLER: It's the smell of history.

THE ENGINEER: They don't even take the trouble to bury them.

The PORTER *comes in.* RAIM, *the interpreter, follows him, blustering and bombastic. He pretends not to deign to glance at the group of travellers.*

THE PORTER: (*as he enters*) The interpreter's just coming.

RAIM: (*off*) Where are they? Foreign slaves and spies, that's what they'll be. (*Entering*) Where are the reactionary traitors?

THE ENGINEER: (*amiably*) You can see that we are not reactionaries. We are nothing of the kind.

RAIM: Then you must be filthy loyalists; a lot of monarchist swine.

THE ENGINEER: I assure you you're mistaken.

RAIM: You're enemies of the people. What have you come up here for? We fight and die, up here! Have you come up here to spy on us? Are you trying to smuggle currency across the frontier?

THE ENGINEER: We are ordinary peaceful travellers. Our papers have been inspected and stamped over and over again. I must ask you once again to rest assured that we are all sympathisers with the League of Councils.

RAIM: (*satirically*) Oh, yes, I knew you'd say that. You're a lot of exploiters, all of you. (*He drops his voice a little.*) And stuffed to the neck with money, I'll bet.

THE ENGINEER: No, sir.

RAIM: Poor little things. No money. We shall see about that.

THE ENGINEER: Not one of us has any money above the permitted amount.

RAIM: Gold, then? Valuables.

THE ENGINEER: No, sir. We all have permission to travel. We merely wish to be allowed to proceed on our way. On the lorry.

RAIM: I'm afraid you'll find that lorry's been requisitioned.

A silence.

THE ENGINEER: Shall we . . . be able to go on . . . by any other means?

RAIM: The road's blocked. In any case the bridges have all been blown up.

A silence.

THE ENGINEER: In that case, will you allow us to go back again to our families?

RAIM: Oh, yes, *I'm* sure! You people, you come up here, and poke your noses into everything, and then go back home and tell tales. I've a pretty shrewd suspicion you'll have to wait here.

THE TRAVELLER: And what shall we be waiting for?

RAIM: The requisite inspections.

THE TRAVELLER: Has anyone authorised you to speak in this way?

RAIM: Has anyone authorised you to poke your nose in?

THE TRAVELLER: On what precise powers do you base your right to interfere with our movements?

RAIM: My powers are my duties as a good citizen of the republic. I act for the republic. And you? What are you waiting for? Show me your hands. Come on.

THE TRAVELLER: (*holds out his hands.*)

RAIM: Proper priest's hands, aren't they just? *You've* never worked for your living. A bishop at least, I should say.

THE TRAVELLER: Your own hands seem to be very well-kept ones too.

RAIM: Thanks, your reverence, very clever, aren't you? Yes: a great pianist's hands, mine are. A pity I can't play. (*He laughs, and turns to the* PORTER.) Orazio, collect these people's documents.

The PORTER *begins to collect the documents.*

THE TRAVELLER: Will *you* be examining them?

RAIM: They'll be inspected by Commissar Amos. We're expecting him any minute. Or better still, General Biante. He'll be here as well, very soon. Yes! Amos and Biante! Are those gigantic figures big enough for you?

THE TRAVELLER: Quite.

RAIM: In the meanwhile, let me hear you say very clearly the word: purchase.

THE TRAVELLER: Purchase.

RAIM: Centre.

THE TRAVELLER: Centre.

RAIM: Now say: January.

THE TRAVELLER: January.

RAIM: Can't say I like your accent very much. You wouldn't be a dirty refugee, by any chance?

THE TRAVELLER: Your own accent isn't particularly good either, if I may say so.

RAIM: Ah, but I'm the interpreter, your reverence. I'm unfortunately obliged to soil my lips with foreign expressions. See? Give me this man's papers, Orazio. (*After a pause*) You claim to have been born in the High Redon, I see.

THE TRAVELLER: Yes.

RAIM: Are you a Slav?

THE TRAVELLER: No.

RAIM: Your surname looks like an alien's to me. Are you a catholic?

THE TRAVELLER: No.

RAIM: Orthodox? Protestant? Jew?

THE TRAVELLER: I haven't decided yet.

RAIM: Good: but I shouldn't take too long about it. Do you live on investments?

THE TRAVELLER: No.

RAIM: Do you own large estates?

THE TRAVELLER: No.

RAIM: Gold?

THE TRAVELLER: No.

RAIM: Bonds?

THE TRAVELLER: No.

RAIM: What are your political opinions?

THE TRAVELLER: I cannot deny that I feel a certain concern for the Queen.

A silence. Everyone has turned to look at him.

RAIM: The Queen?

THE TRAVELLER: The Queen.

RAIM: Good. We'll see how you like trying to be funny when Biante and Amos get here. (*Rudely, to another of the travellers*) You. Show me your hands. (*To another*) You.

The person in front of him is a timid, shabbily-dressed peasant-woman. She puts out her hands, at which he glances in disgust.

RAIM: Peasant. (*Turning to the* PORTER) Even peasants can travel all over the place, these days! (*Turning back to the travellers, with his finger pointing*) You.

He stands there speechless, with his finger still pointing. He is facing a rather attractive woman, with crumpled but not unpretentious clothes, and badly dyed hair. She has hitherto remained hidden among the other travellers. She stares at him: and slowly puts out her hands.

ARGIA: (*in quiet tones, half-teasing and half-defiant*) I have never done a stroke of work in my life. I have always had a very large number of servants at my disposal.

They have all turned to look at her. RAIM *stands there embarrassed, and seeking some way out of his embarrassment. He turns abruptly to the* TRAVELLER.

RAIM: You, sir: *You*, I mean!

THE TRAVELLER: (*politely*) Yes? Is there something else I can . . .?

RAIM: I've been thinking: I didn't like the way you . . . your manner of . . .

THE TRAVELLER: Yes?

RAIM: (*still trying to recover his self-possession*) I'm afraid this ... this casual manner of yours demands closer attention. And the rest of you too: I shall have to go into things in more detail. We must get these things straight. Orazio, you'll bring these people into my room ... in small groups ... or better perhaps, one by one, separately. Yes. These things have to be dealt with quietly, calmly. (*He has gone over to the door. Turning back*) I'd like you all to understand me. You mustn't think I'm doing all this out of spite. On the contrary, you'll find I'm really a friend. It's a devil's cauldron up here: everything in a state of confusion. All sorts of different people ... different races and languages, infiltrators, priests with beards, priests without; everything you can think of: this spot here's a picture of the whole world in its small way. There's too much friction everywhere. Why shouldn't we all try to help one another? Rich and poor, poor and rich. What I mean is, I should be very happy if I could ... assist any of you. Orazio, send them all in to me. (*He goes out.*)

THE PORTER: (*after a very brief pause*) Well, come on. You first ... and you.

He points first to one, then to another of the travellers. They follow RAIM.

THE ENGINEER: Well, it's just as I said: another inspection.

THE PORTER: (*with a quick glance at* ARGIA) Yes. They've been tightening things up since this morning.

ARGIA: (*lighting a cigarette*) But are they really looking for somebody?

THE PORTER: Well ... there's a lot of gossip flying about. (*He casts another furtive glance at her.*)

ARGIA: Is it . . . the so-called "Queen" they're after?

THE PORTER (*evasively*) That's what people are saying.

THE ENGINEER: My dear fellow, all this talk about the woman they all call the Queen, just goes to show what a ridiculous race of people we are.

ARGIA: (*smoking*) I thought the clever lady died, five years ago?

THE TRAVELLER: (*intervening*) Yes, so it's said. But the ordinary people still maintain that in the cellar at Bielovice the body of the woman was never found.

THE PORTER: They were all of them in that cellar to begin with: when they were alive: ministers, generals, and so on.

ARGIA: And was she there too?

THE TRAVELLER: (*to* ARGIA, *with detachment*) Yes, she was. Haven't you ever heard about it? It's quite a story. It's claimed that when the soldiers poured their machine-gun fire down through the barred windows, they instinctively omitted to aim at the woman. So that after the job was finished, under all those bloody corpses . . .

THE ENGINEER (*sarcastically*) . . . the cause of all the trouble was unharmed.

THE TRAVELLER: (*to* ARGIA, *as before*) There were four soldiers on guard at the Nistria bridge, up in the mountains. In the evening a woman appeared. She was covered in blood from head to foot. The soldiers said: "Where are you going?" She looked at them, and said: "Are you sure you have any right to ask me that?" The soldiers said they had orders to stop everyone, especially women. She said: "Are you looking for the

Queen?" "Yes," they said. She looked at them again, and said: "I am the Queen. What are my crimes?"

ARGIA: She wasn't lacking in courage.

THE TRAVELLER: No. She spoke with such calmness, and went on her way with such dignity, that the soldiers didn't recover till the woman had disappeared into the woods.

THE ENGINEER: Very moving. And from then on, according to you, in a country like this, with more traitors than there are leaves on the trees, that woman has been able to stay in hiding for five years?

THE TRAVELLER: Very few people actually knew her. She always remained in the background.

THE ENGINEER: (*ironically*) It's a pretty little tale. In any case what reasons would such a woman have now for springing up out of the ground? Events have passed her by. All the parties either hate her or have forgotten her, which is worse. And why do you call her the Queen? She was never that. Even her most slavish accomplices never flattered her to that extent.

THE TRAVELLER: (*gently*) All the same, the common people have taken to calling her by that name.

THE ENGINEER: The common people have always been fascinated by the major gangsters. Especially blue-blooded ones. That great lady was not only the blazoned aristocratic wife of a usurper; she was the real usurper and intriguer herself. She was the evil genius behind everything, the Egeria, the secret inspirer of all this country's disasters.

THE PORTER: (*suddenly, in an unjustifiably sharp voice, to two more of the travellers*) The next two, please, go along, in there. What are you waiting for?

The two travellers go out. Only the PORTER, *the* ENGINEER, *the* TRAVELLER, ARGIA, *and the* PEASANT-WOMAN *are left.*

THE PORTER: (*to the* ENGINEER) I ... I hate that woman, too, of course. I hate her more than you do.

THE TRAVELLER: (*as though to himself*) All the same, she must have had *some* sort of sway over people.

THE PORTER: People who talk about her say she ... did seem very proud and haughty, but at the same time ... sincere. They say people could never bring themselves to tell lies to her.

THE TRAVELLER: (*with detachment*) The only human needs she ever seems to have acknowledged were the ones that can be reconciled with a dignified and honourable idea of the world. Everything she did and said was, as it were, essential and refined. It must be costing her a great deal to stay in hiding.

THE ENGINEER: Forgive my asking: but did any of you ever see her in those days? (*To* ORAZIO) Did you?

THE PORTER: No.

THE ENGINEER: Have you ever spoken to anybody who'd ever seen her?

THE PORTER: No.

THE ENGINEER: You see, then? It's all popular ignorance: a spirit of opposition prepared to raise even a ghost against the idea of progress, if it can.

THE TRAVELLER: It's a very remarkable ghost, then. (*A pause.*) I'd like to meet it.

RAIM *bursts into the room.*

RAIM: I'd like to know what you all think you're

doing? You take all this very calmly, don't you? The general has been sighted.

THE TRAVELLER: (*calmly*) Indeed?

RAIM: (*to the* PORTER) You, quick, take all these people in there; try and fix them up in there somehow . . . (*To* ARGIA) No, not you. You wait in here. There are some things I have to ask you.

The ENGINEER, *the* TRAVELLER *and the* PEASANT-WOMAN *go out into the next room, at a sign from the* PORTER. *The* PORTER *picks up their documents, which have been left on a table.*

RAIM: (*severely, to* ARGIA) And in particular I should like to know what are the exact and precise reasons . . . the, ah, the reasons why you have undertaken this journey up here.

ARGIA: (*adopting the same official tone*) Personal reasons.

The PORTER *is on his way out of the room.*

RAIM: What were they? I may as well say that it will be as well for you if you explain them in detail.

The door closes behind the PORTER.

ARGIA: (*slowly dropping the official tone*) The reasons in detail were as follows: I was getting horribly miserable down in Rosad, my darling, and I didn't know what to do.

RAIM: I suppose you think it's very clever, coming up here?

ARGIA: They told me you were up in the mountains.

RAIM: What do you want with me?

ARGIA: So now you've joined up with the Unitary

Party, Raim? Clever boy. Are you fighting? Shooting people?

RAIM: I asked you what you'd come for.

ARGIA: Nothing. You should have seen your face when you saw me. I could have died laughing. Have I upset you?

RAIM: (*harshly*) Not at all, I was very glad to see you.

ARGIA: I wonder what your present bosses would say if anyone told them who the ones before were.

RAIM: That's not the sort of thing *you* can feel particularly easy about. When did you leave?

ARGIA: Yesterday.

RAIM: Have you any money?

ARGIA: . . . A certain amount.

RAIM: (*sarcastically*) Yes, I dare say.

ARGIA: I sold everything I had. Not that it fetched much.

RAIM: My dear girl, this is the very last place you should have come to. I only managed to get fixed up here by a miracle. I've had to tell them the most incredible tales. You needn't think I'm going to start running any risks, now.

ARGIA: I will make you run risks, Raim.

RAIM: No, my dear, we're a bit too near Rosad for that. I've enough risks of my own to run; too many. You're a woman, you always get along somehow. But these bloody fools up here, they suspect everybody. The slightest thing, and they're foaming at the mouth. I want to come through all this mess alive. And rich. Yes. What you want up here is a good memory: for afterwards. That's all you want: it'll be a good investment. One side's going to come out on top after all this; and if you've been robbing and betraying and murdering on that side you'll be a hero; if you've done the same for the other you'll be ruined. And there are so many people living in fear and trembling, I've decided to be one of the landed gentry in my old age. If it's anyhow possible you and I can meet up again in the spring. May I ask why you came up here to find me? (*Sarcastically*) Do you love me? Did you miss me down there?

ARGIA: Raim, I really didn't know what to do. The other day, the police arrested me.

RAIM: Why?

ARGIA: They were just rounding people up. I hadn't done anything. I was in a café on one of the avenues. It's difficult now, being a woman on your own.

RAIM: So what?

ARGIA: Oh, nothing. I was actually rather a success at the police-station. I had to stay the night there to start with; but the superintendent was quite kind to me in the morning. He told me to ring up someone who'd vouch for me. Raim: it was then I realised something for the first time: I don't really know anybody. I know people: but they're only Christian names or nicknames, as a rule. I hardly know anybody by their surname. And now, with all this confusion, so-and-so run away, so-and-so dead ... There I was, with the telephone-book, turning over the pages ... and I could think of no one.

RAIM. So what?

ARGIA: They questioned me about my means of subsistence. The result was I was given repatriation notice. The superintendent told me I had to be decentralised, whatever that is. He said they'd send me away the next day with a military escort. "All right," I said: "but I'll have to pack my bags." They sent me home with a guard. I gave the guard my watch, and he pretended to lose me in the crowd. There were no trams, of course; the streets were all blocked; soldiers everywhere; "no stopping here". And so on. Finally, I managed to get a seat on a lorry; the price was sheer robbery. It was raining, my feet were hurting, my clothes were soaking wet; do you know what I felt like, Raim? A rat, a drowned rat. Then at Bled they made us détour, then again at Nova. Inspections. And then more inspections; hold-ups; bayonets. At Sestan they stole my coat. It hasn't been easy getting up here. I'm lucky I've found you so soon. (*She has seated herself on his knee.*)

RAIM: (*getting up*) I'm sorry, my dear, but the people here mustn't know I know you. I'm speaking for your own good as well as mine.

ARGIA: Raim, I couldn't stay down there. I was frightened; can't you understand? Not that they can really charge me with anything. But everywhere you go ... (*with a sudden cry, which she quickly suppresses*) you see the gallows, Raim. Just because of stray accusations ... or vague resemblances, rows of people have been hanged....

RAIM: And you think that's going to encourage me to keep you here? I've as much cause to be worried as you have. It would be madness just to slap our worries together. No, Argia, no: everyone has to look after himself; I want to finish this war above ground, not underneath.

ARGIA: (*after a pause, with an effort to make it seem*

unimportant) Raim: what if I told you . . . that I'd really . . . missed you?

RAIM: That's what I said. You love me. I've bewitched you.

ARGIA: Oh, I know you're quite right to laugh at me. (*Lightly imploring him*) But . . . when we're both together I feel . . . a bit safer. . . . I was happy, when I saw you; don't you understand?

RAIM: Well, I wasn't, see? I wasn't.

ARGIA: Raim. . . .

RAIM: My dear . . . I've no intention of burdening myself with you. Besides, you'll be sure to find a way out, I know you. (*Shrugging his shoulders*) There aren't many women round here. They're in great demand.

ARGIA: (*lowers her eyes for a moment; then looks at him and says, in low quiet tones*) What a disgusting creature you are, aren't you, Raim? I sometimes think you must be the nastiest person in the world.

RAIM: Ah, now you're talking sense. You go away and leave me, my dear; I'm not worthy of you. I'd feel guilty at keeping you here.

ARGIA: And to think that *I* am running after somebody like *you*, begging . . . from *you*. It's enough to make one weep; or laugh.

RAIM: Well, you laugh, then, my dear. Let's both have a good laugh, and say goodbye. You'd be wasted on me. You know, Argia, one of the reasons you don't attract me is your silly games of make-believe the whole time. You've always tried to act so very grand. With me! The superior lady, always disgusted, so easily offended. You of all people! Always behaving as though dirt was something that only belonged to other people.

ARGIA: (*her eyes lowered*) No, Raim, that's not true.

RAIM: While the truth is that if ever there was a filthy creature in the world, you're it.

ARGIA: I'm sorry, Raim, if I spoke like that ... It's only because deep down I love you, and want to ...

RAIM: You let me finish. I'm not angry; not at all. But you may as well get this straight. You see, Argia: you're not only a dead weight on me.... It's not only that. You've begun to get rather too many wrinkles for my liking....

ARGIA: (*trying to turn the whole thing into a jest*) Really, Raim? A few minutes ago, when they were all talking about the Queen, did you know they all looked at me? They half-thought I was the Queen.

RAIM: You! The Queen? They've only got to look at you to see what *you* are. The Queen. There isn't a square inch about you that's decent.

ARGIA: (*with another hoarse effort at playfulness*) Be quiet, Raim, if you don't, I'll bite you! (*She takes his hand.*)

RAIM: (*freeing himself with a brutal jerk which makes her stagger backwards*) You leave me alone. Don't try and pretend I'm joking. What you ought to do, my dear, is to go and stand in front of your looking-glass and say to yourself as often as you can: "I'm a cheap, low, dirty slut." You've never done a decent thing in your whole life. (*Deliberately*) Smell of the bed. Cigarette-smoke. Wandering about the room with nothing on, whistling. That's you. And there have been one or two unsavoury episodes which even suggest that the secret police made use of you. Oh, make no mistake, I'm not the kind of man who's easily prejudiced. But you, Argia, quite apart from everything else, you're cheap. The little bogus middle-class girlie, who's read a few books. Even in your intrigues you're small and petty: the little tart with the furnished rooms and the pawnshop tickets: I've been getting fed up with you now for quite a long time, see? Well: it's over. I'm not going through all that again.

ARGIA: (*her eyes lowered; and with a faint wail*) Raim, I've nowhere to go.

RAIM: Then go to hell. It's the one place . . . (*His voice suddenly reassumes its official tone. He has heard footsteps coming.*) It's absolutely necessary for . . . for political reasons. And even if you have to stay here tonight, it's no great disaster. You and the other woman, that peasant-woman, can stay in here. The other passengers in the other rooms. It'll be all right. I'll see about finding some blankets for you. Political and military necessities, unfortunately. It isn't my fault.

It is the TRAVELLER *who has come in.* RAIM *has turned to him on his last words. The* TRAVELLER *approaches amiably.*

THE TRAVELLER: Nor ours either. I seem to get the impression that you, too, regard these . . . these military and political necessities, with a certain amount of scepticism.

RAIM: (*looks at him for a moment: and then says, also amiably*) Bless my soul, that's exactly what I was saying to . . . (*To* ARGIA, *sharply*) You may withdraw, madam. Go in there with the others.

ARGIA *goes out.*

RAIM: (*amiably but cautiously*) Yes, I was just saying that . . . well, of course, I'm a good revolutionary and all that (we all are, of course), but I . . . understand things. I know how to put myself in another man's place. Unfortunate travellers . . . perhaps even important men, well-to-do, plenty of money and so on, suddenly finding themselves . . .

THE TRAVELLER: Reduced to hoping for a blanket!

RAIM: (*carefully feeling his way*) I'm afraid I may have seemed a little bit . . . official with you just now. I had to be, of course. You understand.

THE TRAVELLER: I have the feeling that you too understand. . . .

RAIM: Oh, at once, my dear friend, straight away. I'll be happy to be of any help, if it's at all possible. . . .

THE TRAVELLER: The secret is to regard these things with a certain amount of detachment; don't you agree?

RAIM: Definitely. You know, I got the impression, when we were talking here a few minutes ago, that you too . . . feel a certain distaste for some of the excesses that . . .

THE TRAVELLER: Ah, you noticed that, did you?

RAIM: Oh, but of course! I'm a man . . . who doesn't feel so very bitter as all that towards your *own* ideals, you know, sir.

THE TRAVELLER: Is that so? I'm delighted to hear it.

RAIM: (*mysteriously*) I'm too much in contact with the new chiefs the whole time, of course.

THE TRAVELLER: (*shaking his head*) And they . . .

RAIM: (*laughing*) . . . aren't so terribly different from the old ones.

THE TRAVELLER: That was to be expected.

RAIM: Once you ignore the individual differences of

character, you find they raise their voices, ring the bell, upset people and shoot 'em . . .

THE TRAVELLER: . . . in exactly the same way as the others. Yes. I assume you were also in the habit of hob-nobbing with the former high-ups?

RAIM: Oh, no, God forbid. I had to put up with them. And now I have to put up with these. "Put up!" It's all very sad.

THE TRAVELLER: Especially for men of intelligence. (*As though speaking to himself*) Who really ought to be looking after themselves.

RAIM: (*warmly*) Exactly! That's just what I say. These disturbances ought to be a godsend for people with any imagination . . .! (*He has taken a bottle out of its hiding-place, and is pouring out a drink for himself and the* TRAVELLER.) "Ought to be looking after themselves." Yes. As you say. Look after yourself, what? You know, I have a theory about all these things.

THE TRAVELLER: I'd like to hear it.

RAIM: There are two kinds of people in this world: the people who eat beef-steaks and the people who eat potatoes. Whose fault is it? Because it's certainly not true that the millionaire eats a hundred thousand beef-steaks.

THE TRAVELLER: (*drinking*) He'd soon have indigestion if he did.

RAIM: (*also drinking*) He eats half a beef-steak and helps it down with a dose of bicarbonate. Yes. Then why do all these other poor devils have to make do with potatoes? It's simple. There aren't enough beef-steaks to go round. The limitation on the number of beef-steaks in the world is a profound inconvenience on which social reforms have not the slightest influence. Not the slightest. Now, it follows from this that whatever régime you're under, the number of eaters of beef-steak . . .

THE TRAVELLER: Remains constant.

RAIM: Exactly. And the wonderful thing is that the beef-steak eaters are always the same people. They may *look* different, of course. But who are they?

THE TRAVELLER: The bosses . . .

RAIM: . . . and the wide-boys. It's always the same act; the palaces and the armchairs are always there, and it's always by virtue of the people and the potatoes that the high-ups can sit in the palaces eating their beef-steaks. That being agreed, what's the logical thing to do? It's to belong, whatever happens, to . . .

THE TRAVELLER: The beef-steak party.

RAIM: It's not for everybody, of course. It requires intelligence . . . intuition. (*With sudden firmness*) You'll forgive me, sir, but I don't believe in equality; except over toothpicks. It's only by climbing up and down that we keep fit. (*Gently*) I believe in money.

THE TRAVELLER: You're not the only one.

RAIM: If man had never developed that great vision of having a bank account, he'd never have emerged from cave-life.

THE TRAVELLER: (*solemnly*) Progress. Progress.

RAIM: A little bit of salt on the tail. Just think what a colossal bore it'd all be otherwise. Everybody stuck there as though in a morgue. A row of coffins. If a man's a hunchback, he's always a hunchback. We all know that. If a man's ugly, he's ugly. If he's a fool, he's a fool. But at any rate, however common and unfortunate a man may be, he can always hope to get rich, little by little. Rich. Which means he won't be ugly any more, nor a fool . . .

THE TRAVELLER: Nor even a hunchback.

RAIM: That's your *real* democracy; your real progress. Yes, that's why it's the duty, the absolute duty of every intelligent man . . . (*his voice changes once more and becomes peremptory and severe; footsteps are approaching*) to fight and to strive! To fight and strive in the service of our flag and our republic! (*He turns to see who is coming in: and is at once thrown into great agitation.*) Good God, it's you, General Biante, forgive me, I never saw you come in! (*He runs to the door.*) How are you? Are you feeling a little better?

BIANTE *has entered, supported by an armed guard,* MAUPA, *who at once helps him to sit down.* BIANTE *is a hirsute man in civilian clothes. His shoulders, neck and one arm are voluminously bandaged, and compel him to move stiffly. He looks first at* RAIM, *then at the* TRAVELLER, *and then turns back to* RAIM.

BIANTE: (*his voice is low and hoarse*) What are you doing?

RAIM: (*eagerly*) Nothing, general, I was just interrogating a traveller.

BIANTE: Oh. Good. And what did the traveller have to say to you?

THE TRAVELLER: (*sweetly*) We were discussing some rather curious offers of help he'd just been making to me.

RAIM: I? General Biante! (*He sniggers.*) I was just holding out a little bait, just wriggling a little hook about. I ought to say that this gentleman seems to me a very suspicious character. I think we should do well to point him out to Commissar Amos ...

BIANTE: (*between his teeth, not amused*) Don't be a bloody fool.

RAIM: ... the minute the commissar arrives.

THE TRAVELLER: (*calmly, to* RAIM) I arrived an hour ago. I am Commissar Amos. How are you, Biante?

BIANTE: Haven't you managed to get me a doctor?

AMOS: Not yet.

BIANTE: I'd be damned glad of one. I come through the whole war safely: and what do I have to be wiped out by? A stray bullet. Amos, I'm swollen right up to the neck; my fingers feel like sausages. I wouldn't like to die, Amos. I'd like to live and see the new age in. Do you think I'm getting gangrene?

AMOS: (*calmly*) Let's hope not.

BIANTE: (*suddenly to* RAIM, *hysterically*) Go and find a doctor, for Christ's sake! You filthy bastard, go and find a doctor! And send all those people in here!

RAIM *rushes out.*

BIANTE: (*breathing laboriously*) The Queen's here! Somewhere: in our midst. Nobody's doing anything, nobody knows anything. And yet they're all saying it! The Queen's here!

AMOS: (*calmly*) Yes, I'd heard for certain she was.

BIANTE: Good God. Who from?

AMOS: They stopped a man on the road from Bled. He was coming up here to meet her.

BIANTE: Where is he?

AMOS: He was too quick for us. While they were

bringing him here. He poisoned himself. So as not to have to acknowledge his accomplice.

BIANTE: (*almost a whisper*) The Queen's here! Alive!

MAUPA: (*suddenly, from the background, without moving, in a kind of ecstasy*) We want to see the colour of the Queen's entrails.

RAIM *is escorting the travellers into the room.*

MAUPA: (*continuing without pause*) All our troubles come from the Queen. If our sick are covered with wounds, if our children grow up crippled and our daughters shameless, the Queen's to blame, no one else. (*His voice gets gradually louder.*) If she falls into my hands, I'll keep her dying slowly for three whole days. I'll make them hear her screams from the mountain-tops. I'll slit her up bit by bit till she lies there wide-open like a peach. The thought that the Queen is near makes my hair stand on end like a wild boar's. We must find her.

AMOS: (*calmly*) She will be found soon enough. The road up here has been blocked since this morning, but the number of road passengers they've stopped hasn't been very large. This very night we shall begin to go over them methodically.

BIANTE: (*turning to the others, who are standing huddled together in the background*) Yes, you there! It's you we're talking about! (*Shouting and getting up from his chair*) I'm here: General Biante. I assume full powers . . . together with Commissar Amos here. . . . Is there anybody here who's a doctor? No? Blast you. (*Brief pause.*) You're all under arrest! No one's to move an inch from where you are now.

AMOS: The exits are all guarded; the guards have orders to shoot.

BIANTE: You'll all be questioned. So look out! You'll be detained here till further orders! (*Pointing*) The women in there; the men in here. Get on with it, everyone to his proper place. (*He moves towards the door.*)

AMOS: (*calmly, for the pleasure of contradicting him*) The men will go in there; the women will stay in here.

BIANTE *casts a sharp glance at* AMOS, *and goes out, supported by* MAUPA.

The travellers have all gone out again except ARGIA *and the* PEASANT-WOMAN.

AMOS: (*also on his way out, turns in the doorway*) Good-night for the present. (*He goes out.*)

ARGIA *stands for a moment looking at the door, and then shrugs her shoulders.*

ARGIA: What a lot of stupid nonsense! The result is that we sleep in here. Let's hope the interpreter remembers to bring us some blankets. There was a sofa in that other room too. (*She points to the next room.*) I'm very tired, aren't you? (*She sits.*) What a lot of clowns they all are. Let's hope they let us sleep till tomorrow morning. (*She begins to fumble in her hand-bag, and brings out a small pot; she takes some cold cream on one finger and dabs it on her face. To the* PEASANT-WOMAN, *who is still seated in the background*) I suppose in the country you don't go in for this sort of thing? I have to, every night: I'm not so young as I was, I've just been told; it would be asking for trouble if I didn't look after myself. (*She massages her face.*) I suppose I must look a sight with this grease all over my face? Sorry. (*She thinks for a moment.*) I find it rather humiliating being a woman. Even rather humiliating being alive. (*She massages her face.*) You spit in a blackguard's face, and even as you do it, you know perfectly well the only thing to do is to make him go to bed with you . . . I'm sorry: but we're both women, after all. I don't mean one really wants to, even. It's all so squalid and humiliating. (*She breaks off.*)

RAIM *crosses the stage and goes out.*

ARGIA: I've come a long, long way just to go to bed with a man. (*Pause.*) Making a fuss of a man to try and find out if he's in a good mood or not. Very amusing. (*Pause.*) The trouble is having no money either. Let's hope after we're dead there'll be nothing of that to worry about. (*Turning to the* PEASANT-WOMAN) Do you mind my asking, dear: I suppose you haven't a bit bigger mirror than this? What . . . what's the matter? Aren't you feeling all right?

THE PEASANT-WOMAN: (*almost inaudibly*) Yes . . .

ARGIA: (*going over to her*) Why, you're covered with sweat. Do you feel ill? You look as if you're going to faint.

THE PEASANT-WOMAN: No . . . no. . . . (*She sways.*)

ARGIA: (*supporting her*) Did what that brute in here said about the Queen frighten you? You mustn't take any notice of that, it's nothing to do with us . . .

She breaks off; lets the woman go; and stares at her. The woman stares back at her with wide-open eyes; then she rises, slowly.

ARGIA: (*after a long pause, in a different voice*) Is there anything you want?

THE PEASANT-WOMAN: No . . . no. . . .

ARGIA: You could go and lie down in there, on the sofa. Where is your bag?

The PEASANT-WOMAN *grips her bag, as though frightened by* ARGIA'S *words.*

ARGIA: What have you got in there?

THE PEASANT-WOMAN: Some bread....

ARGIA: Well, my dear, you go in there. Lie down. You'll soon feel better.

ARGIA *helps the woman into the next room. After a moment she returns, and walks about for a moment or two, perplexed and thoughtful. Suddenly she runs to the other door, opens it and calls in a stifled whisper:*

ARGIA: Raim! Raim! (*She comes back, and waits.*)

RAIM: (*enters: in a whisper*) What d'you want? Are you mad?

ARGIA: (*whispers*) I'm rich, Raim. I'm worth marrying now. Look at me: I'm a splendid match.

RAIM: What's the matter?

ARGIA: Rich, Raim. Rich. We'll be able to stay in the grandest hotels.

RAIM: What do you mean?

ARGIA: I've discovered the Queen. (*She points towards the next room.*)

RAIM: But there's only that peasant-woman in there.

ARGIA *nods.*

CURTAIN

ACT TWO

Only a few moments have passed since the end of the preceding scene. ARGIA *and* RAIM *are speaking rapidly, in low voices.*

RAIM: (*sweating and agitated*) God damn the day I ever met you! You're the cause of all my troubles. This is a frightful thing . . . it's terribly dangerous.

ARGIA: (*mockingly*) Well, why not go to Amos and Biante, then, and tell *them* about it? Tell them the Queen's here; with a heavy bag.

RAIM: Yes, and you know what they'll do? Kill me; and you too. So that they can have the credit . . . and the bag as well. It's a murder-factory up here. Their only aim here is to kill people. Yes: accidentally; for amusement.

ARGIA: Then we'd better forget about it, that's all.

RAIM: I could box your ears! This is the first piece of luck I've ever had in the whole of my life. It's my big chance. I shall go mad if I have to let this slip through my fingers.

ARGIA: Well, don't let it, then.

RAIM: God, I'm frightened of this. A rifle can go off all by itself up here. Damn the whole bloody world! But are you sure about this, Argia? You've always been half-crazy; you imagine things the whole time.

ARGIA: I'm quite certain. We looked at one another. It was just a flicker. And then I saw. And she saw that I saw. She was almost fainting.

RAIM: The devil is there's not a minute to lose. What was this bag like?

ARGIA: Small; but quite heavy.

RAIM: Gold; diamonds. It'll kill me. You couldn't get a needle out of this place. Bury it; come back later: some hopes! They're more likely to bury *me*. (*In a burst of anger*) I'm the one who's in danger, can't you see?

ARGIA: But I can help you. I can do it for you.

RAIM: Yes. You're a woman, of course. You know her ... You've already been talking to her ... But, mind, it would have to look as if it were your own idea. Something you'd thought of yourself. How did she seem?

ARGIA: Terrified.

RAIM: Yes, that's the way to go about it, obviously. Try and frighten her. She'll give you the bag herself, without even being asked.

ARGIA: We mustn't bother too much about the bag, Raim.

RAIM: Why not?

ARGIA: We couldn't be seen with it; and it would be difficult to take it away, or bury it.

RAIM: Well, what, then?

ARGIA: The names.

RAIM: What do you mean, for God's sake, what names?

ARGIA: The names: of her friends. There's sure to be a whole gang round her. Big, important people.

RAIM: By God! You clever piece! (*He kisses her.*) Do you think she'd talk?

ARGIA: We can try and persuade her to. Her life's in our hands.

Raim: You could manage that all right, if you frightened her. But what then?

Argia: We won't take the bag away with us. We'll take the names. In our heads.

Raim: Yes, but surely we could try and get the bag as well? And what if we got the names?

Argia: Well, from then on there'd be quite a number of people who might be feeling extremely uneasy . . .

Raim: (*completing the sentence*) . . . and every so often the tax-collector would drop in and see them. Yes. Me. "Excuse me, your Excellency, you won't forget the usual donation, will you? Though only, of course, if you're interested in surviving a little longer . . . Yes?" My God, what a game! No. No. No! It's too dangerous. It's a good idea, but sooner or later, they'd have me done in. Don't you see? (*With bitter nastiness*) The bastards would soon be sparing *me* the afflictions of old age, don't worry! No, no, Argia, we must try and grab what we can out of it, quickly. Jewels, rubies, and so on . . . (*He suddenly lowers his voice.*) God, here she is. Go on: see what you can do.

The Queen *has opened the door, and stands looking, as though hypnotised, at* Argia; Raim *casts a glance at her and goes out in silence.*

Argia: Did you want something?

The Queen: (*breathing painfully*) No . . . no . . . I only wanted . . .

Argia: To come and talk to me for a bit? Is that it?

The Queen: I . . . saw that perhaps . . . you have a kind heart . . .

Argia: Well . . . that always depends how God made

us, doesn't it? Come over here, my dear. Come on. I wanted to talk to you as well. You're a country-woman, aren't you?

THE QUEEN: (*almost inaudibly*) Yes ...

ARGIA: I'm fond of country-people. Do you actually go out in the fields?

THE QUEEN: Yes ...

ARGIA: What do you do there?

THE QUEEN: I work ...

ARGIA: Digging? Hoeing?

The QUEEN *holds out her hands appealingly.*

ARGIA: Yes, they're real peasant's hands, aren't they? Good girl. It can't be easy to get your hands like that. It must take a long time. And a good deal of hard work. A good deal of digging and hoeing.

THE QUEEN: Yes ...

ARGIA: Are you all by yourself?

THE QUEEN: Yes ...

ARGIA: I can see you're very frightened; I think you've every reason to be. It was sensible of you to come to me. As a matter of fact, I could probably help you. And in return you could perhaps be kind enough to do something for me.

THE QUEEN: I ... don't know what sort of thing ... you mean.

ARGIA: (*almost a whisper*) My dear friend, your name isn't Elisabetta by any chance, I suppose?

There is a long silence.

THE QUEEN: (*she can scarcely speak*) No.

ARGIA: Odd. I thought it was, somehow ... However.

(*She raises her voice slightly.*) You're quite sure your name is not Elisabetta?

The Queen: No ... no ... no ... (*She again holds out her hands.*)

Argia: (*a little louder still*) You insist on denying that your name is ...

The Queen: (*interrupting her with a gesture*) My bag is in there. You can have it. I thought you'd want it. (*She points.*) I've hidden it. You can take it whenever you want to.

Argia: Hidden it where?

The Queen: In there. Up above the rafters, in the corner.

Argia. Is there much in it?

The Queen: Only what I have left. It's hidden in the bread. There are three little loaves.

Argia: It's not really much of a sacrifice for you, is it? If you ever come to the top again, it'll be a mere trifle to you. And if you don't, it's all up with you anyway. But it would be a god-send to me. You see, I'm poor; I'm hag-ridden with debts ... (*She breaks off.*)

Raim: (*coming in quickly*) Excuse me, ladies! I've just remembered about the blankets ... I came to see if ... (*He goes up to* Argia, *and speaks to her under his breath, almost with fury.*) I've been thinking. I want the names as well. I want everything. (*Retreating*) I'll bring you the blankets, in half a minute. (*He goes out.*)

Argia: Yes, you've shown a good deal of common sense. Well, you'll have to show a little more now. The situation is very simple. I can either go out of that door and call a soldier. Or I can keep my mouth shut, and help you. I've a friend here; you just saw him. But I'm afraid it means sharing things out, your majesty. We're sisters now. Everything in common. I'd be a fool to be satisfied with the leavings in the middle of three small loaves, wouldn't I?

THE QUEEN: (*almost inaudibly*) I've nothing else.

ARGIA: For year after year you used to walk on marble and sleep in silk. I've not had quite such a good time. The moment's come to level things up.

THE QUEEN: I swear to you I've nothing else.

ARGIA: That's not true. You still have friends. People working for you. I want them to be my friends as well. I want them to help me. *I* want people I can rely on, too. Do you see what I mean?

THE QUEEN: Yes . . .

ARGIA: In any case, the people I mean are hard-boiled enough. They're the people who've shoved you into all this mess. It was they who drove you out of your hiding-place.

THE QUEEN: No, no, there wasn't anybody.

ARGIA: Your friends.

THE QUEEN: I haven't any.

ARGIA: Come, come, you won't be doing *them* any harm. The only trouble they'll have is helping me a little in these hard times. Your friends.

THE QUEEN: (*imploring*) They're all dead, they've all been killed. I'm alone now.

ARGIA. Your majesty, you used to sweep down red-carpeted staircases; the ones I had to climb weren't half so pretty. But even they taught me things. I learned . . . a good deal. You'll be very silly if you try to fool *me*.

THE QUEEN: Oh, please have pity. . . .

ARGIA: I'm hardened, your majesty. I'm indifferent even to my own misfortunes by now; you can imagine how I feel about yours. (*Almost shouting*) Come on, tell me who they are: who are your friends? Who are they? (*She breaks off.*)

The QUEEN *has taken from her bosom a piece of paper; she offers it to* ARGIA.

ARGIA: (*before taking it*) They're there?

THE QUEEN: Yes.

ARGIA: (*taking the paper*) A good many stories about you are going the rounds. I thought I should have to insist much harder. You're rather meek and mild, for a Queen, aren't you? (*She looks at the paper.*) Darling, you must take me for an idiot. A list of them, all ready? Just like that?

THE QUEEN: Yes.

ARGIA: You've been carrying it about on you?

THE QUEEN: Yes.

ARGIA: (*sarcastically condescending*) Why, my dear, why?

THE QUEEN: Because I'm frightened.

ARGIA: Of what?

THE QUEEN: (*desperately*) Of being tortured. I've heard of them doing ... terrible ... dreadful things ... And I'm frightened; don't you understand? (*Overcome for a moment*) The thought of it is driving me insane! (*Controlling herself*) I'd have been bound to tell them in the end just the same ... And if there was this paper ... They'd have found it on me; it would all have been simple. Oh, please believe me, I beg of you, please. It's the truth.

ARGIA: (*looks at the paper.*) So these are the ones? Your faithful friends. The people who are risking their lives for you.

THE QUEEN: Yes.

ARGIA: (*dropping her voice*) But are you really the "Queen"?

THE QUEEN: Yes . . . Except that I . . . lost whatever courage I had, in that cellar, at Bielovice. Please: I've nothing else to give you now. I hope you'll save me . . . I hope you and your friend will help me to escape . . .

RAIM *enters quickly with a couple of blankets.*

RAIM: Here you are, ladies, the blankets! (*He throws them on a chair; to the* QUEEN) Do you mind? (*He takes the paper from* ARGIA's *hand, and draws her aside. He looks at the card, and says quietly*) It's so stupid and childish it's bound to be true. (*He stares at the paper hard: then puts it under* ARGIA's *eyes.*) You fix these four names in your head as well.

ARGIA: Yes.

RAIM: Good. Have you got them? You're sure?

ARGIA: Yes.

RAIM: So have I. (*He lights a match and sets the paper alight; to the* QUEEN) Madam, we have to think of our safety as well, though our methods may be a bit different. (*He stamps on the ashes hysterically.*)

ARGIA: (*a whisper*) Do you think it's possible to get her away?

RAIM: (*a whisper*) It's not only possible, it's indispensable. And it's not only indispensable, it's not enough. Escape isn't enough. There's something else as well.

ARGIA: What?

RAIM: (*rapidly*) If she gets across the mountains and gets in touch with those people (*he points to the ashes*) it'll go very hard with us. And if she doesn't, it'll be even worse: they'll catch her; and she'll tell everything. And if we leave her here, when they question her to-morrow, she'll talk just the same. She'll give us away. I'd be a madman to risk my life—and yours—on a damn silly thing like that.

ARGIA: What then?

RAIM: We've got to make *sure* she keeps her mouth shut.

ARGIA: (*has understood.*) No!

RAIM: It's the best thing for her too, in a way. If those two in there find her, her last minutes aren't going to be very enviable. She's finished now, either way. Better for her it should all be over quickly without frightening her.

ARGIA: No, no.

RAIM: (*in an excited whisper*) Do you think I like it? Our lives depend on this. We can't back out now, it's too late. We oughtn't to have started it. Darling, it's got to be done.

ARGIA: (*horrified*) Got to? And do you think *I* . . .

RAIM: It's always you, isn't it? Whose idea was it? Yours. You got me into this danger. You arranged it all. And now it's not nice enough for you. You're worse than anybody. No, my dear. It's got to be done. And we're in it together.

ARGIA: (*with horrified resignation*) Have you thought . . . how?

RAIM: I'm thinking now. (*Moving away and speaking louder*) I'll be back in a few minutes, madam. We're looking after you. (*He goes out.*)

THE QUEEN: Does he intend to help me?

ARGIA: (*without looking at her*) Yes.

THE QUEEN: Your friend will get me away?

ARGIA: Yes.

THE QUEEN: (*suddenly, torn with anguish*) For pity's sake, don't let them hurt me, don't betray me, for pity's sake ... (*She darts forward and takes* ARGIA's *hand as though to kiss it.*)

ARGIA: (*almost angrily, tearing her hand away*) What are you doing? What's the matter with you?

THE QUEEN: (*desperately*) Oh, my God, you're deceiving me, everybody deceives me ... Everybody plays with me like a cat with a mouse ... I can't go on any longer; oh, God, I'd rather die now ... I don't want to think any more; call them, call the soldiers, I'll call them myself, kill me, kill me, straight away ...

ARGIA (*shaking her*) Stop it, stop it, you silly woman.

The QUEEN *has fallen to her knees and remains there gasping for breath.*

ARGIA: (*exasperated*) You'll dirty your knees, your majesty. Yes, of course, you'll be saved, you'll be got away. It's important to us as well, isn't it? (*With gloomy hostility*) In any case, it's dishonourable, it's unfair, to lose your dignity like this. It's against the rules of the game; it embarrasses people. A chambermaid would behave better. I would myself, my dear; I've never squealed like that: like a mouse under a peasant's foot. And I'm not a queen ... far from it. When you used to give your orders, with the flag flying over the palace, down below, underneath all the people who were obeying you and giving your orders to other people, down below all of them, right down on the pavement, there was I. I didn't drive in a landau; and they'd made a woman of me by the time I was eleven. Your majesty, there were some days when I used to feel as if the whole world had wiped their feet on my face. And now you come and slobber all over my hands. No, no, my dear: the silk clothes and the box at the Opera have to be paid for. You heard a few minutes ago, in here, what the people think of you. Your hands have not always been rough. And they've signed a lot of papers in their time.

THE QUEEN: No.

ARGIA: What do you mean: no?

THE QUEEN: I've never done any harm to any one. It was never left to me to decide anything. Nothing they say of me is true. (*She shudders with horror.*) The only thing that's true is that at Bielovice I was covered with dead bodies and blood. I could feel them dying, on top of me! Since then I've been in perpetual flight. It isn't true that I met the soldiers on the bridge at Nistria. If I had, I should have fainted at their feet. I've not had a single moment free from terror for five years. They've killed almost every one of my friends; but unfortunately not all of them. Every so often one or other of them manages to track me down. I'm running away from my friends even more than from my enemies. What can they want of me any more? I can't do anything, I don't want to do anything, the only thing I know now is fear; I sleep in fear, I dream in fear. I'll never, never do anything again either for anyone or against anyone. I only want to escape, and never see or know anything again. I want to stop being afraid. Nobody can have anything to fear from me. I'll give up everything, rights, titles, I'll forget everything.

ARGIA: (*with sombre irony*) It almost looks as if I'd done you a service in taking your jewels off you. You are abdicating. There are some people who'd be extremely disillusioned if they could hear you.

THE QUEEN: I have nothing and I no longer want anything.

ARGIA: Then why are you making so much fuss? What *do* you want?

THE QUEEN: To be left alive. Nothing else. Unknown; far away. And to sleep, night after night, in peace.

The two women turn round. RAIM *has entered, slowly. He bows slightly to the* QUEEN, *and beckons* ARGIA *aside.*

RAIM: (*whispers*) The job's going to be taken off our hands. I've found a way out. It's quite respectable, too. This building has two exits: this one, and that one over there. The guard on this one, across the courtyard, will be me. The one on the other, on the wall, is Maupa, that soldier you saw in here. He's a real brute. (*To the* QUEEN) Yes, this is for you, madam. We are preparing a way out for you. (*To* ARGIA *once more*) It was easy to persuade that swine that the revolution demanded that he should fire; often; at sight; the first squeak of a door or movement in the shadows. Even me, if I tried to: if I opened that door, I'd be opening my own way to hell. But that I shan't do. In a few minutes' time you'll hear a signal: the hoot of an owl. The Queen will say good-bye to you, and come out through this door. Our hands will be as white as snow.

ARGIA: (*horrified*) And if the shot doesn't kill her?

RAIM (*gloomy, subdued*) In that case, I . . . (*He breaks off.*) It would be just reckless cowardice to leave the thing half-done. What should I get out of that? The only profit there, would be for my dead bones, because it's obvious the Queen would talk and I'd lose my life. But if a dead man's bones know nothing about profit and loss, do you think stupidity and superstition are going to hold my hand back? Why light candles if your prayers mean nothing? (*He blows to left and right as though to put out two imaginary candles burning before a non-existent shrine.*) They're all wolves: why should I be a lamb? Plenty of good people are dying in these hard times, one more or less makes no odds. They say the bible-stories prophesy a bath of blood for the earth. But in practice it needs gallons, especially when you see how much the earth soaks up. Besides, I suffer from poor health; I've got to make sure of some sort of a future. (*He returns to the subject.*) So if anything goes wrong . . . Oh, why does this woman get people into such a mess instead of doing away with herself? Her life's useless and wretched and short, anyway. Better for her to finish here than run about, being smelt out like a hare the whole time, always in fear and trembling. (*To* ARGIA) If anything does go wrong, as soon as I hear the shots, I shall run round through the courtyard . . . and if the soldier's shots haven't been enough . . . I'll finish it off myself . . . Let's hope it won't be necessary. Quickly, now. I shall be glad when it's all over. (*He makes a slight bow to the* QUEEN *and goes out.*)

ARGIA: (*avoids looking at the* QUEEN.) Madam, you must be very brave now, this is going to be very dangerous for all of us. But I think you'll be all right.

THE QUEEN: I am ready.

ARGIA: (*breathing heavily*) What has to be done, has to. That's true, isn't it? If you want to escape ...

THE QUEEN: Go on.

ARGIA: They've found a man who's willing to accompany you up the hidden paths as far as the frontier. In a few minutes we shall hear a signal. Then you'll go out, through that door over there. Outside, you'll find the man who's willing to take you on your way. You'll have nothing more to worry about.

THE QUEEN (*her hands clasped*) Oh, my dear. Your sweet face and your gentle voice will stay in my heart till the last day of my life, and beyond. Yes, surely beyond; so that when I meet you again in heaven, I can run to you, crying ... (*She takes* ARGIA's *hands.*) "Bright soul! My dear, dear sister! Do you remember me? It is I. And now we are together because on that day we had to part so soon."

ARGIA *tries to push her away.*

THE QUEEN: Don't push me away from you; oh, please let me stay like this for a moment. (*She laughs.*) Treat me like a frightened animal who has sought refuge in your lap. That does happen sometimes. Hold me and stroke me. (*She clasps* ARGIA *tightly.*) What is your name?

ARGIA: Argia.

THE QUEEN: I feel as if I were being re-born, here, in your arms. (*She starts.*) What's that? Was it the signal?

ARGIA: No, not yet.

THE QUEEN: But please tell me: are you sure the man who is going to come with me up the mountain is really to be trusted? Can I really be sure of him? When we get to one of those dark gullies in the hills, he won't leap at me and cut my throat, will he?

ARGIA: No. No.

THE QUEEN: Don't, don't think I don't trust you. It's only that it is so difficult to shake off the terror. Through the whole of these years I've been haunted by only one single thought: the horrible tortures they do ... My God, they put people to inhuman horrors: did you know that? I have a poison with me ... but I can never be sure if I shall be able to swallow it in time. I always used to imagine that dreadful moment: a man looking at me ... turning round to look at me ... then a glint in his eye ... and I was recognised ... lost. That's why I've ... oh, dearest Argia, please forgive me! But you said yourself we were women together ... (*Whispers*) Sometimes a man has stared hard at me ... a peasant, or a herdsman, or a woodman ... I've given myself to him! Given myself! I'm no longer either a queen or a woman. (*Weeping and laughing*) I'm like a terrified animal running this way and that. Argia: I've had a baby too, up in the mountains. You're the first person I've ever told.

ARGIA: Is that why you're going? You want to see the baby again?

THE QUEEN: Oh no! No! No! Why should I want to see him? Why should I love him? No, no, he only pursues me like all the rest. I'm running away from him as well. I don't want to see him. He can only be another threat to me. Let him stay where he is, and grow up in peace. (*She bursts into sobs.*) And may God forgive all of us.

ARGIA: Don't shake like that, my dear. Try and be calm. You'll be all right.

THE QUEEN: (*whispering and laughing*) Argia, I even think I'm . . . pregnant again. I keep feeling so hungry the whole time.

ARGIA: (*looks at her, and gently strokes her face*) You're covered in sweat. Wipe your face.

The hoot of an owl is heard outside.

THE QUEEN: (*starting*) That's the signal, isn't it? And now I have to go.

ARGIA: Wait a moment.

The signal is heard again.

THE QUEEN: Yes, it's the signal. Good-bye, Argia. Let me kiss you. (*She kisses* ARGIA *and gets ready to go to the door.*)

ARGIA: Wait.

THE QUEEN: Why do you say wait?

ARGIA: I didn't explain properly. That's not the way you must go out. They'll shoot you, if you go through that door.

THE QUEEN: What then?

ARGIA: It's through this other door. You must go through here. I've thought of a better plan.

THE QUEEN: How?

ARGIA: I'll push the door open on this side . . . oh, there won't be any danger. All I'll have to do is to push the door; they're such fools, they'll fire at once. The men on guard over that side will run round as soon as they hear the noise. That other door will be unprotected. You must seize the moment, and get away.

THE QUEEN: Shall I find the man there—the man who's to go with me?

ARGIA: No. Make for the mountains by yourself. You were probably right, it's safer that way.

The signal is heard again.

ARGIA (*pointing*) Stand ready, over there. Quietly.

The QUEEN *fumbles for a moment, and gives* ARGIA *a ring.*

THE QUEEN: This was the last burden I had ...

ARGIA: (*putting it on*) It's tight on me. So I shan't lose it.

The QUEEN *goes and stands ready near one of the doors.* ARGIA *puts out the lamp; takes a pole, makes a sign of encouragement to the* QUEEN, *and goes cautiously over to the other door. She moves the door with the pole, and suddenly throws it wide open. A deafening burst of machine-gun fire splinters the door.* ARGIA *laughs silently. She makes a sign to the* QUEEN.

ARGIA: Now! Go ... Good-bye.

The QUEEN *slips out.* ARGIA *stands waiting.*

VOICES: (*outside*) On guard! On guard, there! Look out!

MAUPA: (*coming in with his gun in his hands: to* ARGIA) Don't you move!

ARGIA: You're irresistible.

MAUPA: And don't speak.

ARGIA: Oh, I wouldn't know what to say to you, anyway.

VOICES: (*distant*) On guard! On guard!

ANOTHER VOICE: On guard!

RAIM: (*enters breathlessly*) What's the matter?

MAUPA: This woman was trying to escape.

RAIM: My dear fellow ... haven't you made a mistake?

MAUPA: I tell you she tried to get away! Perhaps you doubt my word?

RAIM: No, no. I'm sure you're right.

MAUPA: You watch her. I'll go and call the others. (*He goes out.*)

RAIM: (*greatly agitated*) What's happened? Where is she?

ARGIA: Gone.

RAIM: What have you done, you fool? And what are you going to tell them now?

ARGIA: I shall think up something; don't worry.

RAIM: Just you see you don't bring me into it ... You needn't count on me ... You'll get yourself out of it, I don't doubt ... (*He breaks off at the sound of footsteps; turns to the newcomers; and says with emphasis*) Sir, this woman was trying to run away.

AMOS: (*has entered, followed by* MAUPA. *He turns quietly to him.*) Friend, will you please point that gun downwards? We've no need of it.

MAUPA *does so.*

AMOS: (*to* RAIM) And you, will you give the lady a seat?

RAIM *does so.*

AMOS: (*politely to* ARGIA) Will you please sit down, madam? You wanted to go out?

ARGIA: I was thirsty.

AMOS: Ah, that explains it. You'll forgive us. At all

events the incident has one good side to it. It offers us (*he points to* BIANTE, *who is coming in supported by the* PORTER) an opportunity of asking you to be good enough to grant us an interview . . . which I hope will be quiet and friendly. It's an opportunity I was looking for during the whole of our journey.

BIANTE: (*coming forward and shouting*) Light! Light! We might as well be in a cave! Bring some candles and lamps! Give us some illumination worthy of our cause.

RAIM, MAUPA, *and the* PORTER *have already rushed out to fetch lights from the neighbouring rooms. The first to return is the* PORTER, *with a strong lamp. Its light falls on* ARGIA. *There is a moment of curious silence.*

AMOS: (*to* ARGIA) Madam: what is your name?

CURTAIN

ACT THREE

Only a few seconds have gone by. RAIM, MAUPA *and the* PORTER *are still bringing in lamps, and arranging the room. Then they all sit.* ARGIA *is standing in the midst of them.*

AMOS: Well?

ARGIA: (*with hostile indifference*) You will find my name, and everything else about me, in my documents. I have already been questioned once this evening, with the other travellers. Is this extra honour reserved for me alone?

AMOS: Madam: we have to ask you for a little further information.

ARGIA: There is no need to address me as madam. I'm only one of those very common plants you naturally find growing on the manure-heap of three wars.

AMOS: What is your nationality?

ARGIA: I was born in this country. And from that day to this, people like you have done nothing but repatriate me, expel me, deport me, search me, give me notice to quit; and so forth.

AMOS: (*coldly polite*) You sound as though you considered *us* responsible for all that.

ARGIA: Well, what are you doing now, if not giving orders? There are a great number of people in the world who've made it their job to decide what the rest of us have to do. Congratulations. You might tell me what it feels like.

AMOS: Have you never known what it feels like?

ARGIA: I? (*She pauses a moment, surprised.*) I? (*With a shrug*) I've always been one of the people who take orders, not give them. It's my job to be here submitting to them, at this time of night; when I'm dropping with fatigue.

AMOS: Political necessities.

ARGIA: Ah, yes, political necessities: they're the reason we're forbidden to eat what we choose, every other day; the reason we're forbidden to go to bed when we're tired, or to light the fire when we're cold. "Every time is the decisive time." And how brazen you all are about it! It's been going on since Adam. Political necessities.

AMOS: Have you never used those words on your own behalf?

ARGIA: (*surprised*) I? My dear friend—you will forgive the expression—I've already told you that I've never done anything very useful or respectable in the whole of my life. Satisfied?

AMOS: What occupations have you followed up till now?

ARGIA: Oh, various ones. What I could pick up. You, and others like you, have always been so busy shouting that I've never had much chance to think about my own condition. There have been times when I've not been sorry if I could find someone willing to pay for my lunch or my dinner.

AMOS: Can you prove that?

ARGIA: Witnesses? Certainly, darling, certainly. Lots of men know me. I can prove it whenever I like.

BIANTE: (*sneering: his voice is like a death-rattle*) Have you any distinguishing marks on your body to prove your identity? Little things . . . that might have struck the attention of the men who paid for your lunches and dinners?

ARGIA: (*after a pause; in a low voice*) Yes. Men like you, and men even more repellent than you, if possible, have seen me and made use of me. That is what I am.

AMOS: (*quieting* BIANTE *with a gesture*) You don't seem to like us very much. Is there any special reason for that?

ARGIA: Yes: I always dislike the authorities: people who walk over our faces the whole time; and have rather a heavy tread.

AMOS: (*still politely*) Madam: I should perhaps convey to you some idea of the impression you are creating.

ARGIA: Well?

AMOS: The sharpness of your answers is in rather striking contrast with the humble condition you declare yourself to be in. And the bluntness you attempt to give those answers is in equally striking contrast with your obvious refinement and breeding.

ARGIA: (*after a pause*) Refinement and breeding? In me? You think I look . . .? (*She laughs.*) How nice. You're trying to make love to me.

AMOS: I also have the impression that the liveliness of your behaviour is largely due to your need to conceal a certain amount of fear.

ARGIA: Fear? I?

AMOS: Yes.

ARGIA: Fear of whom? Of you? I realise that the contempt people feel for you makes you try and console yourselves with the idea that everyone's frightened of you. But I'm not frightened of you; why should I be?

I've told you what I am. And I can prove it, whenever I choose.

BIANTE: Why not now?

ARGIA: Because just at the moment, I happen to be enjoying myself. Yes, it's odd, isn't it? I'm actually enjoying myself.

BIANTE: Let's hope you go on enjoying yourself.

AMOS: (*imperturbably*) If your insolence fails to conceal your fear, your fear seems to be equally unsuccessful in curbing your insolence.

ARGIA: (*ironically*) I wonder why?

AMOS: Pride.

ARGIA: You think I'm proud, do you?

AMOS: Yes: with a pride which won't even listen to your own common sense when it warns you. You are scarcely even taking the trouble to lie successfully. What you would really like at this moment is to tell us you despise us.

ARGIA: (*taking out a cigarette*) As a matter of fact, it does strike me as slightly unnatural that people like you should give yourselves airs.

BIANTE: You'd better be careful, my dear; he was trained for the priesthood.

AMOS: An ancient pride which has soaked right through to your veins. Footsteps, used to the echo of surroundings where the press of the crowd is unknown. Hands, accustomed always to holding bright and precious objects; a voice that never had any need to raise itself in order to call for silence.

ARGIA: (*after a moment's reflection*) And that's what your intuition tells you about me, is it? All that?

AMOS: Madam, you are doing yourself a great deal of

harm by lying to us. Suppose you come down to earth? Where were you born?

ARGIA: (*is silent for a moment; then she laughs, and shrugging her shoulders, says with insulting sarcasm*) I was born in one of the finest mansions in the city. I won't say whether it was on the first floor, or in the porter's lodge. In my room, when I woke, I always saw nymphs on the walls. The tapestries had hung there for five hundred years. Yes, you are right: I did, indeed, grow up among people who were silent the minute I indicated that I was about to speak. And when they answered me, it was always in pleasant voices, saying pleasant things. (*Mockingly*) I walked on carpets as large as a village square! The doors were always opened for me! The rooms were always heated: I have always been sensitive to the cold. The food was excellent; I have always been rather greedy. My dear friend, you should have seen the tablecloths, and the silver! The crystal goblets I used to drink from!

AMOS: And all this good fortune cost *you* very little trouble.

ARGIA: (*in satirically affected tones*) We don't ask the rose what trouble it has taken: we ask it simply to be a rose: and to be as different as it can from an artichoke. They used to bring me whatever I wanted on beautiful carved trays; then they would bow and retire, always turning at the door and bowing once again before they went out. (*Indicating her cigarette*) Do you mind?

AMOS: (*going across and lighting it*) And why did you insist on their doing all that?

ARGIA: I didn't insist. They wanted to. And you know, I think you too, if I were to smile at you, would also wag your tails. But no, the price would be too high: for me, I mean. Your arrogance is simply your way of bolstering yourselves up. And I . . . (*She breaks off.*)

AMOS: (*in lighting the cigarette, has noticed the ring.*) That's a very beautiful ring you have there.

ARGIA: (*tries to remove it, but cannot.*) It won't come off. (*Lightly*) I've been wearing it too long. It's a family heirloom. (*She looks for a moment at them all; then laughs, with mocking bitterness.*) Yes; in my time, I've been a proud woman . . . rich . . . highly respected, elegant, happy . . . fortunate . . .

AMOS: (*coldly*) And your political opinions?

ARGIA: I'm not interested in politics.

AMOS: But at least you prefer one party to the other?

ARGIA: Do you?

AMOS: Yes.

ARGIA. Then I prefer the opposite one.

AMOS: Why?

ARGIA: For the simple reason that I don't like the way you behave. You strut about a great deal too much. (*With derisive affectation*) You see, ever since I was a child I have been brought up to respect people of a very different sort from you. People who washed properly, and wore clean-smelling linen. Perhaps there's some political significance in that? I can't believe that an unpleasant smell gives people special rights. Or perhaps the revolution has a smell?

BIANTE: The smell of bitter soup in the people's tenements.

ARGIA: (*affectedly*) I'm sorry. I have never smelt it. I think you probably give yourselves too much work to do; you smell of sweat.

AMOS: The stonebreakers and the poor who follow us have less delicate nostrils.

ARGIA: That must be very sad for them.

BIANTE: (*with painful vehemence*) Tomorrow we shall have no stonebreakers and no poor!

ARGIA: (*insolently*) We shall have other troubles. Otherwise what would *you* do? You canalize people's miseries. You turn them first into envy, then into fury. The thick rind of bad temper on the world has grown a great deal thicker since you began to cultivate it. The number of the dead has grown too. And all your great ideas don't prevent a distinct smell of blood rising from you.

BIANTE: Amos, for God's sake!

AMOS: (*cutting him short*) Do you realize where all these questions are leading?

ARGIA: Yes.

AMOS: Is there anyone here who can identify you?

ARGIA: Certainly. Otherwise I would hardly be taking such risks.

AMOS: Who is it?

ARGIA: I'll tell you later. The night is long . . . and so is the mountain-road. Provided *you* have the time to spare . . .

A SOLDIER *has entered, and has whispered something into* BIANTE'S *ear.*

ARGIA: . . . though they do say that gunfire can be heard round about. Bad news? Is that what's worrying you?

AMOS: Don't hope for miracles; they don't happen any more.

BIANTE: Stop it, Amos, make her talk, for God's sake! Make her talk, I'm in a hurry! My body's burning as if it would set the whole bloody world on fire.

ARGIA: (*insolently*) Moderate your voice, please. (*Suddenly and passionately*) If I were the queen . . . If I were the queen, do you know what I would say to you at this moment? (*In a manner not devoid of majesty*) I'd say: "Gentlemen." (*She drops back into a more normal tone, but soon returns to her former manner.*) "Gentlemen, you are angry with me; but I am not angry with you. Neither the power you have usurped, nor your threats, are capable of disturbing me. We are far apart. It is that that makes you boil with rage; and keeps me calm."

AMOS: If you're not the queen, I'm bound to say you give a very good imitation of the haughty way in which she'd behave on an occasion like this.

ARGIA: The reason is that I've been rehearsing this rôle for a very long time. Every time any one has been rude to me—and that can happen to anyone, can't it? —every time I've come away with my cheeks still burning, what scathing retorts, what tremendous, noble answers I've always imagined! I know everything a woman of spirit can say to put the insolent in their places. . . .

The noise of hoarse voices begins to be heard outside.

ARGIA: (*continues passionately*) And if I were the queen I'd say to you: "It's true, gentlemen, there was no mob round me, there was space. The echo used to carry my words on high and purify them . . . make them lonely; and calm. The echo used to liberate them . . . (*Slightly intoxicated by her own words, she plays with the echo.*) Re . . . gi . . . na . . . It made them mount upward . . . up . . . on high . . . high . . . high . . . it wanted them to be calm and just . . . Re . . . gi . . . na . . ."

They have all, one after another, stood up; they stand listening to that echo, and to the distant voices.

BIANTE: (*suddenly*) What's happening? What's the matter, out there? Who are those people coming up the road? Why are we wasting time? My fever's getting worse; I'm burning all over. What are our weapons for? Yes, we do need dead people! What are we waiting for? Are you waiting till I'm dead here in the middle of them? (*To the* PORTER) What's going on out there?

THE PORTER: (*has been out: and now re-enters, distressed.*) General Biante and Commissar Amos! Something's happening. The road out there is black with people.

BIANTE: Who are they?

THE PORTER: The people living in the upper valley. They must have got to hear about this woman, they must have heard she'd been caught, and they've come down under cover of the dark.

ARGIA: I told you, did I not, that your power was only provisional?

BIANTE *is already hobbling quickly out.* AMOS, RAIM *and* MAUPA *follow him.*

THE PORTER: (*remains alone with* ARGIA. *He looks at her; and suddenly, with impulsive reverence, takes off his cap; he is at once ashamed of himself, and pretends to be looking at a sheet of paper on the table beside him. As though reading from the paper: in a low voice*) There are a great many cowards in this world, who are so frightened that they hide their true feelings; and I am the lowest and most cowardly of them all. But for us, more than for others, what comfort and healing it brings, to know that there is someone . . . (*his eyes do not move from the sheet of paper, but his voice rises slightly*) . . . there is someone who is still unafraid, and can stand alone against all the rest! What consolation, for us in our shame, to think that in a soul shaped like our own, everything that in us is ruined, stays faithful and untarnished! To know that such a creature has drawn breath in this world! I believe that even God Himself, hearing her speak, is proud of her. And whoever shall think of her, though it be a thousand years from now, shall feel once more upon his face a look of dignity. (*His voice has become louder, but his eyes have never once raised themselves from the sheet of paper.*)

MAUPA *and* RAIM *come in, holding the door open for* BIANTE.

BIANTE: (*goes up to* ARGIA, *and suddenly bursts into a laugh*) Hahaha! Your Majesty! Yes, your famous name has brought a lot of people down from the mountains to meet you. Do you know what sort of help they're bringing you? Do you know what they want? (*Almost casually*) To see you condemned to death and hanged.

MAUPA: (*with quiet ecstasy*) We want to see the colour of the Queen's entrails.

AMOS: (*entering and raising his hand*) There will be a proper trial. Otherwise we should be showing very little trust in our own purpose.

BIANTE: (*shouting*) Proper trial! Formal procedure! To hell with this chattering. I've no time to waste. I can't feel my own hands any more; I can hardly keep my eyes open.

AMOS: A jury will sit. (*To* MAUPA) You: Go and bring some of those people in here.

BIANTE: (*to* MAUPA, *as he goes out*) And choose people who look sensible, and keep their eyes on the ground!

AMOS: Peasants merely: but now they have authority: optimists, and the world is full of them; in revolutions they are manna dropped from heaven. Every one of them believes that the sickle will cut the whole meadow but will stop a quarter of an inch short of his own throat.

BIANTE: And the jury ought to have a few beggars on it as well ...

AMOS: ... a few people who are stupid and lazy, and imagine that a change in the insignia over the doors will give them the reward of the industrious and the intelligent ...

A number of peasants, men and women, have entered. The ENGINEER *is among them.*

BIANTE: (*to the newcomers*) Come in, my friends! Sit down. You already know that I have taken over the command. That means that everybody can kill a man, but I can do it with a roll of drums, like an acrobat making a difficult leap. The republic has conquered. (*He beats his fist on the table.*) Well then, I preside! (*To* AMOS) You shall be the accuser! (*To* RAIM) You shall write. (*To the newcomers*) You shall judge! (*Lowering his voice*) And after that, I, as president, if I'm still alive, shall carry out the sentence. You can begin, Amos.

AMOS *has already risen: he speaks in the tones of a chancellor reading out an act.*

AMOS: The accusation charges this woman with having concealed her identity, and falsified her papers.

ARGIA: Gentlemen! Please, please listen to me. I came up here ...

AMOS: ... with the intention of fleeing the country? Or to try to discover the whereabouts of your son? Yes, madam, we are fully informed about that also. Your son. (*His voice slightly rising*) She is also accused of having formerly exercised a secret and illicit influence on the heads of the state, inducing them to enact factious and oppressive laws. ...

BIANTE: Oh, get on with it, Amos! You're cold, you've got no guts! You're just being cruel!

AMOS: (*louder*) ... of inciting to massacre and persecution ...

ARGIA: But I have never done anything of the kind!

AMOS: ... of having fomented conspiracies aimed at undermining the authority of the state. ...

ARGIA: But that's what you've done! And you blame it on the Queen! *You* were the sowers of discord.

AMOS (*louder*) ... to the point of inducing a number of fanatics to take up arms against their country.

ARGIA: But I ...

AMOS: This woman is accused of having herself unloosed the present conflict; of having herself driven it to atrocious excesses. She herself summoned to this country foreign armed forces, herself lit the fires that now smoke from every point of the horizon, herself disfigured the dead along the roads. ...

ARGIA: But I tell you I ...

AMOS: ... didn't know? Didn't want it?

ARGIA: I tell you that my hands . . .

AMOS: Are clean? Is that it? That only shows how cunning you've been. It deprives you of extenuating circumstances, if there ever were any.

THE ENGINEER: (*suddenly and violently*) I was walking in the street one day: there was a cordon of soldiers; and they said to me: "Not this way, the Queen will be coming down here." I went round another way, and they told me: "You can't come through here." Everywhere I went, it was the same. Madam, you were always in the way.

ARGIA. Friends, friends, but I was there too, with you: on your side of the cordon, not the other.

A PEASANT-WOMAN: (*suddenly bursting into sobs*) The shirt I washed for my son, he said it was shabby. He said the soup I cooked for him tasted nasty. And now they've told me that he's lying out there, in the fields, with his arms wide-open, covered with ants. It's all the Queen's fault.

ARGIA: You stone that woman now, only because you one day fawned on her!

A PEASANT: (*violently*) When our children are old enough to play games, they're not allowed to play the same games as rich men's children. That's a terrible thing! That's what poisons their minds!

THE PEASANT-WOMAN: My son hated the earthen crockery, he hated the smell of our home; he hated his own life!

THE PEASANT: My daughter went away with the soldiers, and I haven't heard a word of her since. That was your fault!

THE WOMAN: It was your fault!

BIANTE: All of you! All of you! Bear witness, all of you!

THE ENGINEER: It was her fault!

MAUPA: It was her fault!

OTHERS: Her fault! It was her fault!

BIANTE: And what about you? That porter over there! Are you the only one with nothing to say?

(*A silence*)

THE PORTER: Yes . . . everything she did . . . humiliated us.

ARGIA: (*rebelliously, to the* PORTER) And who was it who taught you humiliation and envy? Who was it who let your rancour loose?

AMOS: (*with sudden intensity*) You, the apex of privilege, the symbol of prerogative; you, the emblem of those distinctions from which humiliation and rivalry were born. Your whole authority is based and built upon inequality. It is in you that injustice is personified, it is in you she finds her arrogant features, her scornful voice, her contemptuous answers, her sumptuous clothes, and her unsoiled hands. Your name of Queen is of itself enough to make men see that they are unequal: on one side vast revenues, on the other, vast burdens. You are the hook from which the great act of tyranny hangs. The world will be a less unhappy place when you have vanished from it.

ARGIA: (*remains for a long moment with her head bent.*) Forgive me. I have been play-acting a little: perhaps too much. Now I will tell you the truth. I can prove that I am not the Queen, and I can prove it at once. There is someone here who can witness for me.

BIANTE: Who is it?

ARGIA: That man over there, your interpreter. Stop, Raim, don't run away. He knows me only too well. He knows I'm not a queen. I'm the sort of woman who has to smile at lodging-house keepers, and traffic in pawn-tickets.

RAIM: (*comes forward slowly, in silence.*) There must be some misunderstanding. This woman must be mad. I've never seen her before in my life.

ARGIA: Look at me, Raim.

RAIM: I am looking at you. (*To* AMOS) I've never seen her before.

ARGIA: (*turning to the others*) My friend is frightened things may have gone too far. Whether I'm the Queen or not, or he's my friend or not, he's afraid you just have to have a certain number of people to shoot, up here. He just wants to stay alive, that's all.

RAIM: I knew you'd say that. But I must insist that I do not know you.

ARGIA: Gentlemen! I and this man, who "doesn't know" me, kept each other warm all through one whole winter!

RAIM: Rubbish!

ARGIA: I came up here solely to look for him. There are people here who saw us talking.

RAIM: (*to the others*) Of course they did. I tried to approach her: because I thought she looked suspicious. I don't know who she is. I'm sorry, madam, but I can't help you.

He moves away, disappearing among the others. ARGIA *stands for a moment in silence.*

ARGIA: (*almost absently*) Perhaps it's true. Perhaps that

man and I never did know one another. But, cven so, gentlemen, that doesn't give you the right to make stupid mistakes. If you have to have a corpse to show people, when you tell them the Queen's dead, you might at least look for a corpse a bit more like her. You fools! I, the Queen? Is mine the voice of a queen ...? Has my life been the life of a queen ...? (*Suddenly calling*) Raim! Raim! Call him back!

AMOS: I'd like to bet that your friend is far away by now; and making for the mountains like a hare.

ARGIA: (*bewildered*) Gentlemen, there is someone else who can witness for me. There were two women travellers in this room. I ... and another woman.

AMOS: (*amiably*) Yes. (*He makes a sign to one of the soldiers, who at once goes out.*)

ARGIA: ... a peasant-woman.

AMOS: (*amiably*) Yes. And where is she now?

ARGIA: She ran away. But she can't be far off. That woman ... can tell you ... that I'm not what you think. And you will have what you want, just the same. Send out and look for her.

AMOS: Up in the mountains?

ARGIA: Yes.

AMOS: All you can say of your witnesses, is that one is fleeing and the other has fled. (*A pause.*) Madam, we have a surprise for you. (*A pause.*) Your peasant-woman is here. She didn't get very far. Here she is.

In a great silence the QUEEN *appears, escorted by the soldier. The* QUEEN, *pale, and rather stiff, looks round her.* AMOS *points to* ARGIA. *The* QUEEN *comes forward to* ARGIA; *and speaks to her with a slight stammer.*

THE QUEEN: Forgive me, my dear ... it was all no use ... I knew they'd have caught me ... The moment I was so frightened of ... arrived ... But I don't think ... they've caught me in time ... to hurt me. I managed to fool them ... you know how ... I prefer it ... to be all over at once. Good-bye, my dearest friend. I was so afraid ... but not so much, now. (*She sways, and sinks slowly to the ground.*)

BIANTE: What's the matter?

ARGIA: (*kneels down beside the* QUEEN, *and takes her hand. After a while she looks up, and says, as though lost in thought*) She carried poison with her. (*A pause.*) You have killed her.

AMOS: (*cutting her short*) You are now completely without accomplices. Say something, why don't you?

BIANTE: (*shouting*) You've no-one left now!

AMOS: It's all over with you, your majesty! Answer us! You are the Queen!

ARGIA: (*rises slowly.*) Not every eye shall look to the ground. There shall still be someone to stand before you. Yes. I am the Queen!

A silence.

BIANTE: She's confessed, Amos. Quick, make your speech for the prosecution.

AMOS: (*rises, and thinks for a moment.*) If friction is to be stopped, the only way is to remove the cause; if disturbances are to be brought to an end, the only way is to eliminate the disturber. I see only one way to make such eliminations final.

The witnesses, perturbed by the decision by which they are to be faced, rise cautiously, first one, then another, trying to efface themselves.

AMOS: No other method is known whereby revolutions may be at once prudent and rapid; nor any other argument that makes them so persuasive; nor any procedure which more effectively seals dangerous lips and more finally immobilises enemy hands.

The witnesses have cautiously moved towards the door, but at this point AMOS's *look arrests them.*

AMOS: (*continuing*) Such a method serves also, among other things, to identify the weak pillars; in fact, you will notice that some of our jurymen who have divined the responsibility that is about to face them, are cautiously trying to slip away one by one: they do not realise that, in the course of time, that may render them also liable to furnish proofs of the excellence of the method. It is quite true that the importance of a revolution is in proportion to the number of dead it produces. Biante, it is your duty to pronounce sentence.

BIANTE: (*exhausted and swaying, rises, supported by* MAUPA.) The revolution has decided that the Queen must die. I order . . . I order . . . (*He cannot go on, he has come to the end:* MAUPA *lifts him back into his chair.*)

AMOS: You are no longer in a position to give orders. Your post is vacant. (*He turns to the others.*) The revolution has decided that the Queen must die. The sentence will be carried out during the course of the night.

CURTAIN

ACT FOUR

A short time has elapsed since the previous act. ARGIA *is dozing. In the background, a soldier is asleep on a wooden chair.* AMOS *comes in: he shakes the soldier, and sends him away. Then he wakes* ARGIA.

AMOS: I've come to inform you that the sentence must be carried out very shortly. The messenger who is to take the news of the execution to my government must leave during the night. In fact, we all have to leave this area before morning, for unexpected military reasons.

ARGIA: (*half-absently*) Yes.

AMOS: I also have to tell you that you can discount any possibility of rescue. Any move on the part of the Coalitionists would be ineffective: arrangements have already been made to carry out the sentence at the first alarm.

ARGIA: Was this the only reason you came to see me?

AMOS: No. On the contrary. There is a much more important reason. In fact, you may regard everything that has happened so far tonight as a mere preamble to what I have to tell you now.

ARGIA: Well?

AMOS: Do you really think the revolution would have given so much of its time to your frivolities this evening, and taken so much trouble to give an appearance of legality to the trial, if we had no precise aim in mind?

ARGIA: Well: what is it?

AMOS: The revolution intends to be irreproachable right to the end. I have come to tell you that you are free to ask for pardon.

ARGIA: From whom?

AMOS: From us. Will you ask for it?

ARGIA: (*after a pause*) I will ask for it.

AMOS: Good. The coldness of the night seems to have brought you to your senses. (*He sits.*) Naturally the pardon is dependent on certain conditions.

ARGIA: What are they?

AMOS: Formal ones. Futile even. Before I disclose them to you, I would like you to realise exactly what would happen to you in the event of the pardon being refused. The human mind often seeks refuge in vagueness. However: outside this building is a stone platform. On it, when you went out, you would see six armed soldiers. You would then go and stand in front of them. You would fall. A short while after, the sunrise would illuminate a universe in all respects as usual, except that you would not be there. That is all.

ARGIA: The conditions.

AMOS: The signing of a list of declarations concerning the events of the last few years. The witnesses are ready. (*He turns to the door.*) Come in.

The PORTER *and* MAUPA *come in and remain in the background.*

ARGIA: What sort of declarations?

AMOS: Saying that you acknowledge that you have conspired, etcetera, have summoned foreign help against your country, etcetera, and confess yourself guilty of illegal actions, dishonourable conduct, etcetera.

ARGIA: (*almost indifferently*) They sound like lies to me.

AMOS: You will also be required to give us certain information. But that we can go into later.

ARGIA: Is the paper ready?

AMOS: Here it is.

He makes a sign, and the PORTER *approaches* ARGIA *with a paper in his hand. She turns, and sees him; she has stretched out her hand; now she withdraws it. The* PORTER *puts the paper in her hand.*

AMOS: I forgot to give you one other piece of news. The flight of your accomplice—the so-called interpreter, I mean—was unsuccessful. They had to fire at him; I am afraid he was seriously wounded. In the hope of surviving and winning our clemency, he employed his last moments in betraying you even more comprehensively than he had done before. He confirmed all the allegations made in that document.

ARGIA: (*thoughtfully*) Poor Raim. His eyes were a nice colour; it was pleasant to look into them. How terribly concerned he was to keep them open on the world. In vain, apparently. Good-bye, Raim. This wind is carrying all the leaves away.

AMOS: Yes, madam. It's the time of year. Whole gatherings of people who yesterday sat in gilded halls, could to-day reassemble in hell with no one missing. Your other accomplice, the peasant-woman, was at least able to say good-bye to you.

ARGIA: (*thoughtfully*) She was so terrified; so very unpractical. She wanted to sleep, night after night, in peace. Good-bye.

AMOS: I mean that you are now alone. But alive,

luckily for you. Try and remain so. In times like these, and at so small a cost (*pointing to the paper*), it's a good bargain.

ARGIA: To tell you the truth, I scarcely know any longer whether I want to make a good bargain or not. (*She takes an uncertain step forward; sees the* PORTER *staring at her; and stands still again.*) But, Commissar Amos, you must really think me very simple, if you imagine you can deceive me so easily. No, I know as well as you do that there is no way out of this. (*She gives back the paper to* AMOS.) To survive and to be able to describe such things would be hard enough, even for your witnesses. And think who the chief character is. No. It wouldn't be a very clever move on your part to allow the Queen to go free, so that the common people could come and kiss the hem of her garments while she described to them how you forced her signature from her.

AMOS: A reasonable objection. We had thought of it already. It also explains your courage earlier this evening . . . (*with a faint suggestion of bitterness*) a courage which would have been a very humiliating slap in the face for us, if we hadn't been aware how gratuitous and false and easy it was: as courage usually is, in my opinion. Madam: you thought then that everything was lost already; so your fine gestures cost you nothing. Very well. I've come to tell you that in fact nothing is lost, so far as you're concerned. The revolution has an interest in keeping you alive. (*A pause.*) Alive, and in circulation. Alive . . . (*almost casually*) and in disgrace. Confess. And first you'll be despised; then ignored. And then: no longer a queen, but a woman: a woman, no longer walking on fine soft carpets, but huddled on the hard floor of an all-night bar, learning the pleading smiles of poverty . . .

ARGIA: (*lost in her recollections*) . . . listening to the cheap jokes of the bar-man, with an anxious smile on her face; soothing and flattering the bad-tempered taxi-driver . . . (*The eye of the* PORTER *is on her.*) But who, who on earth, could ever conceive that a woman of such birth and spirit, stainless and honourable, could foul herself by signing such a document? They'll never be willing to believe that.

AMOS: They will have to believe it. We shall give them the proof. I've already told you that you will furnish us with certain information, information you alone possess. On that information we shall act. And the world will be compelled to realise that it was you who gave it to us.

ARGIA: (*with melancholy indifference*) . . . And so . . . poor Queen in disgrace . . . you spare her, and the others cut her throat; her friends.

AMOS: At least it would be time gained. Unless—and this is the point—some of the others, your friends, I mean . . . (*Breaking off: to* MAUPA) You go outside.

MAUPA *goes out.*

AMOS: (*to the* PORTER) You wait over there. (*He turns back to* ARGIA.) I was speaking about the others, your friends: in order that we can take steps to protect you and save you from them, (*dropping his voice*) you will tell us their names. (*With a sudden cry, pointing a finger at her*) Yes! You know them! I saw it! I read it there, in your eyes! They glinted. You've seen the way to save yourself. And you know you have it there at your disposal: inside your head. (*Persuasively*) Well, then, first: it's clearly in the interest of the revolution to keep you alive so that respect for you shall die out. Secondly: it's indispensable that the revolution shall know the names of your accomplices. The two things fit together; and save you. Your disclosures will be the beginning of a great clean-up. There are cold-blooded vipers lying curled up in our very beds. Illustrious personages and obscure imbeciles. Even here, a short time ago; it was quite clear that your fine speeches were directed to someone's ears. They will all be rendered permanently harmless. (*His voice drops to a whisper.*) Who are they? Where are they? What are their names? Quickly: tell me their names.

ARGIA: (*stands for a moment with bent head.*) Your voice went very quiet when you asked me for them, didn't it? If it made you feel sick to ask for them, what do you suppose I should feel if I were to divulge them? (*With a wan smile*) It's obviously not a thing to be very proud of. And unfortunately, I don't know any names.

AMOS: You not only know them: you've already wisely decided to disclose them to me. However, you will no doubt make me wait a little for them; that was to be expected, and I shall not refuse to indulge you. It's a due one has to pay to the concept of honour. You merely want to be persuaded.

ARGIA: (*with a wan smile*) The men you want me to hand over to you, certainly never expected this as their reward.

AMOS: Those men have simply staked everything on one card. In their complete selfishness, they were prepared to make use of you. Do you know any of them personally; or feel affection for any of them? No. Bonds of gratitude? No. (*Ironically*) Is it for some political ideal that you are prepared to sacrifice yourself?

ARGIA: (*almost absently*) I know very little about such things; I've told you that before.

AMOS: Or perhaps the thought of your good name is holding you back? The little plaster figure of your reputation crashing in pieces? Madam: don't take any notice of cant-phrases; follow nature: which fears death, and knows nothing else. Only thus will you be sincere, and therefore honourable. After all, the finest reputation in the world is very little comfort to a corpse.

ARGIA: (*thoughtfully*) Yes.

AMOS: Good. (*Although the room is almost empty, and the silence in it is absolute*) Well, then, gentlemen, silence! The Queen is deciding.

A silence.

ARGIA: So my decisions can actually make people hold their breath. Messengers are getting ready to announce them beyond the mountains.

AMOS: That does not, however, give you one minute's extra time. (*He calls*) Maupa!

MAUPA: (*appearing in the doorway*) Everything is ready.

AMOS: (*dismissing him with a wave*) Good. Tell them to wait.

ARGIA: I am a person who can make people wait. It's the first time that's ever happened to me. I can say yes: I can say no.

AMOS: You have very little time left, madam.

ARGIA: Do not try to hurry the Queen. The Queen. I am only just beginning to realise what it means to be one.

AMOS: It means obeying a few flatterers in order to rule over many subjects.

ARGIA: Not at all. To be a queen really means: to be alone. It means: to have gone on ahead, to have left everyone else behind. Enemies, friends: all gone. A great simplicity. This room is indeed a palace; your aversion from me is only a form of respect; you are only a rebel subject. I can say yes; I can say no.

AMOS: At a price, however.

ARGIA: It is the only one I can pay. (*She suddenly shivers with cold.*) And suppose I decide to pay it? I am free: to say yes, or no. And no one in the world can do anything about it. I am the one who decides. It's beautiful; to be able to talk to you like this; to look about me like this . . . and to feel my breathing so free, and the beating of my heart so peaceful.

AMOS *has taken up the cloak left by the soldier, and places it round her shoulders.*

AMOS: You are shivering.

ARGIA: It is the cold that announces the dawn. The only thing I am afraid of, is getting tired; it's been a wearing night. (*A pause.*) I don't even feel dislike towards you.

AMOS: The technique of pride, is it not? The technique of pride. (*With sudden anger*) But pride is not flesh and blood, madam! The chosen creature's superiority with which you think you can even now keep us at a distance! But it's not your flesh and blood! It's a shell!

A crust, that's all. Born of habit. Like the hardness of the hands of a peasant. But you haven't earned it by digging. It's come to you from the bowings and scrapings of a whole palace all round you since the day you were born! Give me those names. Firmness, honour, eyes that never lower themselves, the technique of pride: I'd like to know what would be left of all that, if you'd had to live in some of the places I've known, and cooked yourself an egg over a spirit-lamp, and gone out of an evening in a greasy overcoat, with a nice smile ready to try and soften the man at the dairy. Yes, yes, our eyes can't look at people as yours do . . . even our thoughts, here inside us, are a bit grubby, and shabby, and common, and bruised by rubbing shoulders with the crowd . . . But don't try to imagine they are so very different from your own. Just lift the curtain a little. Come on, give me the names. If I were to twist your wrist, you'd scream like the rest of us! Your majesty, have you ever seen the little white grubs in rotten meat? They suddenly spurt out, and writhe about furiously. Minute as they are, they want to live; to feed; to reproduce; they do exactly what we do: you: everyone: and in exactly the same way. The proud boast of being a person, a will, someone distinguished, is no more than a matter of fine linen. Take people's clothes away from them; and that's exactly what they'll be. All naked, equal grubs, wriggling about as best they can. The slightest planetary disturbance could quietly wipe everything out. And instead of wriggling as equals, do we have to give one man heaven and another man hell? Come down from your tin-pot throne. Get used to these things. Get used to being reasonable. Let your own instincts win; and be afraid: it's your way of wriggling. Give me those names.

ARGIA: (*her teeth chattering*) What you're saying, in fact, is that if there were here, in my place, some less fortunate woman than I, someone who'd had to cook herself an egg in her room, you're saying that there'd be some real merit in *her*, if she were courageous at this moment? Commissar Amos, there was once a woman whom they played a joke on. I was told about it. One Sunday, this woman went to the seaside. And the bathing-attendants, for a joke, knowing the sort of woman she was, got out for her a bathing-costume of the kind that becomes almost transparent in the water. There was a good deal of merriment. And all of a sudden, the woman noticed that everyone was looking at her, and that there was rather a row going on.

AMOS: Come on: the names.

ARGIA: And at last that woman saw that she was standing there almost naked! Alone and naked. She stood there bewildered. And suddenly, do you know what she did? She tried to laugh, with them. (*Controlling herself, and shrugging her shoulders*) And after all what did they see? That she was a woman. We know what a woman is. A man comes up to her . . . cheerful, with his big, sweaty hands, and says: "Do this . . . go like this . . . do that . . . (*louder*) . . . go on . . ." (*Suddenly, with a real cry of anguish and protest*) Well, do you know what I think! I think there comes a time when the only thing to do is to stand up and say . . . (*as though actually turning on someone*) "Why do you insult me like this? And, my God, why have I allowed you to? Get away from me! Go away! Go away! Leave me alone! You take advantage of an immense mistake, a monstrous delusion! Respect me! Show me respect! Respect ... because I am ... the Queen! The Queen, and destined for other things than this." (*With a change of voice*) What I want to do is to go out of doors, as if it were a fine morning, and as if I had seen down there, at the end of the street, the cool fresh colour of the sea, a colour that makes the heart leap! And someone stops me, and then someone else, and someone else, with the usual rudenesses. But this morning I don't even hear them. I'm not afraid any longer. My face expresses dignity. I am as I would always have wished to be. And it would have been simple after all. It would have been enough to want to be. Palaces have nothing to do with it. It was my own fault.

AMOS: (*after a long pause*) Am I to take this to mean that you still refuse? (*Almost with melancholy*) Very well; in that case, your troubles are not yet over. Madam: you are forcing me to do this, remember.

He goes to the door, and makes a sign to someone outside. MAUPA *enters slowly, leading by the hand a small boy about three years old, dressed in peasant-boy's clothes.*

AMOS: You can go, now, Maupa. So can you, porter.

MAUPA *and the* PORTER *go out. The boy is left standing alone in the middle of the room.*

ARGIA: (*shaken*) Who is he?

AMOS: (*with the same melancholy, moving to the child's side*) It is the person who will persuade you.

ARGIA: (*desperately*) I don't know who he is!

AMOS: I know of course that you don't actually recognise him. We ourselves had a great deal of trouble in tracing him.

ARGIA: (*cries out*) I swear to you! I swear . . . that he isn't my son! I'm not his mother!

AMOS: He's a fine child. He'll be able to live and grow up as an unknowing peasant . . . so long as the protection you are according to a few seditious men doesn't force us to eliminate in him any pretext for sedition in the future. In such an orgy of blood, the scales won't be upset by a few drops more . . . Well, that is what you wanted: to choose: now you can do so.

ARGIA: (*instinctively clutching her face*) He isn't mine! I tell you he isn't mine.

AMOS: It is in your power to choose. The weight of this tiny little boy puts an end to your flights of fancy, and brings you back to earth. Even the wolves in the woods up here love their young. Yes: that's a real thing: the rest is smoke. Make your choice: make it according to nature: no one will condemn you.

ARGIA: (*astounded*) And if I don't, you're capable of a crime like this?

AMOS: (*with lofty sadness*) Madam: I shall do everything that is necessary. Common reproaches should be reserved for common occasions. The blood that your disclosures will make flow may be a great deal, but it will be far away. There is only a little here. But it is warm. And it is your own.

ARGIA: Oh God, how can a human mind have so much hate in it?

AMOS (*with painful intensity*) It is not hate. But it is too late to argue now. I also made my choice once upon a time. However a stone rolls, the one who has dislodged it rolls down with it.

ARGIA: My God, how can you ... break laws so sacred ...? I tell you he isn't mine! Did you keep me alive only to save me for this? I swear to you he isn't mine, take him away, take him away ... Oh God, oh God, how can you think you've the power to ... (*Crying out*) In what name, by what right, do you dare to do this?

AMOS: (*shouting her down*) In what name! By what right! (*Suddenly controlling himself*) Listen to me: I want to tell *you* something also. When we overthrew the October republic, I was in the palace too. An agreement had been reached; our victory was total and peaceful. There had been no bloodshed. All the same, we were in the palace rooms; we wanted to pull down the coats-of-arms. We began to unnail them. A man was fetching great blows at one of the trophies. And I noticed that little by little something seemed to dawn in his face. Down below in the street the crowds were yelling. Suddenly this man, as soon as he'd knocked the trophy off the wall, turned round. He was covered in sweat. And he hurled his axe at one of the mirrors! The others followed suit. Then they began to smash everything. And their faces were furious, they were intoxicated, they were beautiful, they were holy. The smoke was already appearing! And the fire followed! (*Controlling himself suddenly*) But it would have been contemptible if the aim of it all was merely to take a few pence from the hand of a fat dead man and put them in the hand of a thin living man. So much noise simply in order to modify a few tariffs and initiate a few austere apostles into the pleasures of wearing silk shirts? But this fury, which spouts up like a fountain of black oil, comes from deep down, madam, it's the distillation of a very different grief, the memory of a very different betrayal, it doesn't merely utter its "no" to your silks and satins and the farmer's hoard. (*He cries*) It says "no" to everything there is! It says rage towards everything, despair towards everything! What we hear coming towards us down there, is the thunder of the great waterfall! It's towards the great rapids that the boat is rushing! This fury says "no" to the whole world: it says: (*with despairing weariness*) that the world is wrong, it's all absurdity; an immense, unchangeable quarry of despair, a grotesque, unchangeable labyrinth of injustice, an insensate clockwork, that one day compels you and me to say and do what we're saying and doing now. It says "no"; total sterilisation; away with everything: the just and the unjust, loyalty and betrayal, worthiness, guilt, glory: (*He points to* ARGIA.) ... everything that makes us grasping and boastful owners in life and in death, all this mass of falsehoods, this immense fraud! Tell me the names.

ARGIA: (*staring at the child*) The names? But you'll kill him whatever happens, I know you will. (*A brief pause.*) Oh, poor little child, in his little peasant's dress! No one wants him. His mother runs away from him. I've done nothing but say: "Take him away." Completely alone. (*She suddenly runs to the child, and hugs him tightly.*) Oh, what a lovely child you are, my darling. How healthy you are. And what pretty little teeth. My angel, your mother won't ever come and see if you're asleep, she'll never see you run, and say: "Look how he's grown." He isn't at all sleepy, is he, and not the tiniest bit afraid, is he? No, no, he's very well, he's in the warm ... (*She is pressing him against her breast.*) ... This is the right place for a little boy to be, isn't it? This is a little throne for a child ... (*She turns to* AMOS.) Sir, I've been deceiving myself. I thought that everything would be simple. Perhaps I should after all do as you say ... I ought to tell you those names ... I'm so confused ... Wait a moment ... those names ... (*She stands there, with eyes wide-open, looking before her; suddenly she laughs softly; and whispers*) A miracle, sir. A miracle. I've forgotten them! Perhaps I have been too much upset, or perhaps I have been helped in some way; but that step has been spared me. (*She hugs the child tightly, hiding her face against him, and remains thus.*)

AMOS: (*after a long pause*) In that case the struggle between us is over. All that remains is to finish what was begun. (*A pause; then, seriously and gently*) If you believe in the survival of your soul, and desire a confessor, anyone you choose may hear you.

ARGIA: Yes, I do desire it. (*She rises without letting go the child.*) I have made sad and improvident use of my person, my words, my thoughts, and for the most part, of the whole of my life. I laid the blame for this upon others, when the blame was all my own. This I understood too late. I have often told lies; and even now.

AMOS: What is your real name?

ARGIA: I believe that the Lord, in a short time from now, will not be asking names of me; He will be asking what my profit has been. The only one I have had I have had this night. And so, not utterly bereft, but with a little coin I go before Him. (*She raises her head slightly, and her voice also.*) Only a little, but my own; not given to me, nor inherited; but mine. This is the profit that makes owners and possessors of us. I am sinning still; since of what I have done tonight I am a little proud: it is the single thing that I can tell about myself . . . (*Dropping her voice a little*) I have great need that soon I shall meet someone who will listen to me. (*She turns.*)

MAUPA *comes in, followed by the* PORTER.

ARGIA: Now is it?

AMOS: Yes.

MAUPA *goes over to take the child from her.* ARGIA *prevents him, hugging the child close.*

AMOS: (*motioning* MAUPA *to stand back*) The child will return to where he has lived hitherto, and where no one is informed of who he is. (*He takes the child from* ARGIA.) The sentence will be carried out at once. Immediately afterwards, it will be announced that the woman known as the Queen is dead, and that therefore the Unitary Government has triumphed, the actions of our enemies being now deprived of their aim.

ARGIA *moves towards the door, preceded by* MAUPA.

ARGIA: I believe that God . . . has intentionally made us, not docile, for that He would find useless . . . but different from Himself and a little too proud . . . so that we may . . . stand against Him, thwart Him, amaze Him . . . Perhaps that is His purpose. (*She takes another step forward.*) It is a long struggle. Only at the end do we find reconciliation; and rest. (*She looks at the child.*) I go away rich. I have acquired a son . . . and memories . . .

If even a little memory survives in us, this night, for me, shall shine indeed. (*She shows her hand to* AMOS.) Tell them to leave this ring on my finger. (*She holds out a hand to the child.*) Good-bye, my sweet.

The child also puts a hand out towards her. ARGIA *turns to go towards the door; pauses in momentary bewilderment; extracts her lipstick, and puts a little on her lips.*

ARGIA: My mouth was rather pale. (*She is now at the door.*) How lovely and serene it is over the mountains; and the star Diana is still there in the sky. Unquestionably, this is a seat for kings, and in it we must try to live regally.

She goes out. There is a silence. Suddenly the PORTER *runs out after her.* AMOS, *listening, puts his hands over the child's ears.*

A burst of gun-fire is heard. ARGIA *is dead.*

THE END

THE BURNT FLOWER-BED

(*L'Aiuola Bruciata*)

A Play in Three Acts

(1951–52)

CHARACTERS

GIOVANNI
LUISA, his wife
ROSA
TOMASO
NICOLA
RANIERO

A peasant, and four other men
who do not speak.

The time is the present.

THE BURNT FLOWER-BED was performed at the Arts Theatre, London, on September 9th, 1955, with the following cast:

GIOVANNI	ALEXANDER KNOX
LUISA, his wife	YVONNE MITCHELL
ROSA	DUDY NIMMO
TOMASO	LEO MCKERN
NICOLA	ESMÉ PERCY
RANIERO	EDGAR WREFORD
A PEASANT	JOHN NETTLETON

The Play was produced by Peter Hall

The Scenery was designed by Paul Mayo

ACT ONE

The scene, which is the same throughout, represents a room furnished in the normal way, but of unusual structure. At the back, leading outside, there are a number of wide glazed doors, under massive arches. Through them, in the distance, the high peaks of snow-covered mountains can be seen.

The room is empty, and the outer doors are closed. Someone outside is knocking at one of them. GIOVANNI *appears on the lower steps of a staircase; he comes slowly into the room as if he did not hear, and sits down.*

A VOICE: (*from outside*) Mr. Giovanni! There's a gentleman here come to see you. I've brought him up; he wants to speak to you.

GIOVANNI *does not answer.*

He says it's important, urgent.

Further knocks at the door.

GIOVANNI: Push: the door's unlocked.

The door to the west opens. A PEASANT *stands in the doorway. He makes way for the stranger to pass him, and then retires. The stranger,* TOMASO, *comes into the room.*

GIOVANNI: (*after a moment's pause*) Well, well. I never expected an actual visit.

TOMASO: We wrote to you. More than once.

GIOVANNI: Yes, but . . . fancy *you*, coming all the way up here!

TOMASO: (*mildly—it is his usual manner*) It had to be me. I had to talk to you.

GIOVANNI: It must be important then. Sit down.

TOMASO: (*after a pause*) You look very young still. Are you keeping well?

GIOVANNI: Yes.

TOMASO: And what have you been doing all these years? You've been very sparing with your news.

GIOVANNI: Resting. On holiday.

TOMASO: This is the old customs-house, isn't it? Converted.

GIOVANNI: Yes, we're very high up, here.

TOMASO: It must be a bit cut off—especially in winter. The signal-box . . .

GIOVANNI: (*indifferently*) It's down below. But the road's a bad one, fortunately.

TOMASO: Is there anyone here with you?

GIOVANNI: My wife.

TOMASO: She well too?

GIOVANNI: Yes.

TOMASO: No one else?

GIOVANNI: No. (*A silence.*)

TOMASO: And you've elected to live right on the frontier. Did you have this place during the old government?

GIOVANNI: Yes. I liked having a little place only a stone's throw from the border. We used to come here every summer.

TOMASO: And you still kept it on afterwards, under our own . . . *your* own government.

GIOVANNI: Well, why not? The world's in a very disturbed state.

TOMASO: And it looks pretty dark at the moment, don't you think?

GIOVANNI: So they say. (*A silence.*)

TOMASO: And . . . where exactly is the frontier

GIOVANNI: (*indicating it vaguely, without turning*) Up there.

TOMASO: (*opens the east door at the back and looks out.*) Whereabouts?

GIOVANNI: It's all one big meadow. It goes up this side, and down on the other.

TOMASO: A lot of flowers.

GIOVANNI: Yes; they only last a few days. The place is called the Flowering Plain. The same flowers; this side, and that.

TOMASO: All the same, other rivers begin over there, running down the other way; other languages, other ideas.

GIOVANNI: Oh, yes, everything's the wrong way round over there. (*He laughs shortly.*)

TOMASO: Is the road cut off?

GIOVANNI: (*looks at him for a moment.*) Yes, ever since the last war but one.

TOMASO: Does nobody ever go across? Refugees? Or smugglers?

GIOVANNI: Not now.

TOMASO: Is it dangerous?

GIOVANNI: The peasants are careful not to go up there when they're mowing. No, there's just wind and flowers. (*Signs to him to listen.*) Listen . . .

A sound, like the murmur of a crowd, is heard.

TOMASO: Wind?

GIOVANNI: Yes, in the branches.

TOMASO: It sounds like the scraping of feet.

GIOVANNI: It sounds like the scraping of feet. Some seasons it blows from here over to there; others, it blows from there over to here.

TOMASO: And that's all that ever goes across?

GIOVANNI: That's all. Wind . . . and then silence. (*A silence.*)

TOMASO: It's an illusory silence. This spot—up there, the frontier I mean—is the point of attrition between two huge wheels. One half of the world against the other half. Armaments, hate; threatening clouds. The Advisory Council is meeting the day after tomorrow, as I suppose you know.

GIOVANNI: Will you have something to drink? (*He has taken out a bottle and glasses.*)

TOMASO: (*vaguely*) You know . . . we've been needing you, Giovanni.

GIOVANNI: Yes, I think you said as much when you wrote.

TOMASO: We've missed your co-operation a great deal.

GIOVANNI: Something to *do*; that was what was missing. Our ideas had conquered.

TOMASO: (*speaking as he often does, in a tired, amiable monotone*) Yes, but unfortunately it's always the same after a victory. Old friends begin to quarrel with one another. My dear Giovanni, the thing that unseated you was only a little conspiracy. Another little conspiracy could just as easily have put you back again. You oughtn't to have gone off like that; sulking your life away. What happened to you? A man of your stature. You lost your balance; you went off out of spite. It's time we all joined up again.

GIOVANNI: (*vaguely*) No, no, it wasn't spite. I just felt rather . . . sated. Satiated.

TOMASO: You don't think you're the only one? We none of us get any younger, after all.

GIOVANNI: In that case, what do you want *me* for? (*He breaks off.*)

A young woman, LUISA, *has silently entered the room; she nods in response to a bow from* TOMASO; *and then goes over to the glasses, finishes arranging them, pours out the drink, and carefully places small table-napkins beside the glasses.*

GIOVANNI: (*has paused to watch her; now he addresses her affectionately.*) Luisa, this is Tomaso: you used to know him in the old days. He isn't actually in the government; he's more important even than that, and he's done us a great honour in coming all the way up here. If you go out, take care, won't you? It's getting chilly.

LUISA: Do you think I ought to put a pullover on?

GIOVANNI: Yes, it might be as well.

LUISA: I'd like to go out for a little walk.

GIOVANNI: You'll still have an hour before sunset.

LUISA: But I suppose . . . it may be damp? Do you think I'd better stay indoors?

GIOVANNI: (*slightly embarrassed*) Just as you like, my dear.

LUISA: I could read, couldn't I?

GIOVANNI: Yes.

LUISA: I'll go upstairs and read. Or do some work.

GIOVANNI: Yes.

LUISA: By the window.

GIOVANNI: Yes.

LUISA *nods goodbye to* TOMASO *and goes out. After a long silence,* GIOVANNI *turns back to* TOMASO.

GIOVANNI: No, Tomaso, it wasn't spite. It never really bothered me much, being thrown out. You think I ought to come back?

TOMASO: Of course you ought.

GIOVANNI: Yes, of course; naturally. I wonder if I'm still up to it. I was first and foremost an orator, after all: an "orator". I'd be a bit rusty now, wouldn't I? The machine would creak a bit after all these years . . . (*He breaks off on the last word.*)

LUISA, *upstairs, is heard quietly singing the refrain of an old popular song.*

GIOVANNI: (*continuing*) No, it wasn't spite, please don't think that. I was over-civilised, that was the trouble. Too much given to irony. One drop is enough to turn the whole barrel sour. (*He absently hums for a moment the refrain that* LUISA *is still singing.*) Naturally, naturally, we're always here and ready, if it's for the Cause. The Cause. What a great many meanings the word has. The trouble comes when the Cause has won, and we all have to sit down. Peacetime has a way of rubbing the bloom off military leaders. (*He laughs.*) Well, what's it matter? The world's an ungrateful place: people don't like too much care and attention lavished on them. (*He drinks.*) And look at yourself: you have your hands on all the controls. Technique has unified the commands. You may appear small, but actually you're a giant . . . (*After a pause*) If you dump a great brick down on the ground, the first thing it does is squash the grass. You think you're doing people a kindness, and then you find you've offended them. (*A silence.*)

TOMASO: (*who has watched him throughout in silence*) But as a matter of fact, the people remember a great deal about you; do you realise that? Yes. Power in our hands has only had the effect of diminishing us; while this semi-exile of yours has done you a great deal of good. It's you who are the giant. You may not know it, but your name's very much in the air.

GIOVANNI: People are talking about me?

TOMASO: Yes.

GIOVANNI: What are they saying?

TOMASO: You're almost a legend.

GIOVANNI: (*after a pause*) Were they fond of me?

TOMASO: They *are* fond of you.

GIOVANNI: They may be now. They weren't before.

TOMASO: Yes, perhaps they were, even before.

GIOVANNI: "Perhaps." Meaning?

TOMASO: They admired you.

GIOVANNI: They got rid of me just the same.

TOMASO: Exactly. You were too big. Too much in the limelight. But look at me!: I've never been a striking figure. No one ever recognises *me* in the street.

GIOVANNI: What do you mean: too big? Too domineering?

TOMASO: No: too persuasive. A character. You didn't leave much space round you. You made us feel ... rather hemmed in.

GIOVANNI: I bullied people.

TOMASO: (*shaking his head*) You ... got your way.

GIOVANNI: (*ironically*) A bully.

TOMASO: No. You were polite . . . and determined. And subtle, too. You were never cruel, Giovanni, far from it. But the revolution was in danger of becoming *yours*, of having your profile stamped on it, like a coin.

GIOVANNI: What you mean is nobody *really* liked me in fact.

TOMASO: (*a little ironically*) You were adored by the crowds.

GIOVANNI: Yes: I spoke well. (*He smiles.*) Do you think I poisoned their minds? Would you say the people who heard me went away feeling a bit happier or a bit sadder than before?

TOMASO: Your real power lies in the fact that people remember you as someone kindly and benevolent. I don't know if they're right. Your speeches may have had a touch of rhetoric about them; but at least they meant hope, and peace, and brotherhood.

GIOVANNI: Yes, and as soon as people had listened to them, they went away and threw stones. Evidently they failed to assimilate quite all of what I tried to say. And why do you only remember me now?

TOMASO: Because you'd have been no use to us before. (*He quotes, with gentle irony*) "His giant wings make him unable to walk." Politics are always what goes on at the back of the shop. Its major facts are the sum of many small moments: moments too small for the really great men.

GIOVANNI: And now?

TOMASO: Now is the moment for you to come back on to the stage again. History is a superb puppetmaster, she picks her marionettes with perfect timing. Don't think the metaphor's meant to be disrespectful towards you; nor towards me. But at this moment, you're a trump card. We need the man who used to cry for brotherhood and peace. Everything is going according to plan. All by itself. And the moment to play you has arrived.

GIOVANNI: In what way?

TOMASO: (*after looking at him for a moment*) What we want from you . . . most of all . . . is advice.

GIOVANNI: (*with an absent laugh*) You've come up here to try and get me involved again. But I'm . . . (*He breaks off.*) I'm afraid I . . . (*He turns towards the stairs.* LUISA *has stopped singing. He calls up the stairs*) Luisa. What's the matter?

LUISA *appears on the stairs.*

GIOVANNI: Was there something you wanted to say to me?

LUISA: (*pointing outside*) I'm sorry to interrupt you, Giovanni, but just down there, under the trees . . . I wanted to tell you there's a group of people down there. As though they were hiding.

GIOVANNI: (*goes to the back and looks out: to* LUISA) I'll go down and see. (*He turns to* TOMASO.) I see there are quite a crowd of you. So you really have found some use for me. (*He goes out.*)

LUISA: (*to* TOMASO) Do you think he's changed?

TOMASO: Why do you ask?

LUISA: (*after a moment's pause*) I don't think he'll be able to help you. (*A silence.*)

TOMASO: (*approaching her*) What do you mean?

LUISA: Oh, he wouldn't want to mention it himself. He hasn't told you?

TOMASO: Told me what?

LUISA: The reason. The real one.

TOMASO: The reason for what?

LUISA: For everything. The reason we're here; why he's so different now. Did you notice how grey he's gone just here? Poor Giovanni, he's very strong; he doesn't allow much to show. That's why I wanted to warn you. I don't think he'll be able to come back to you.

TOMASO: (*coming close to her; cautiously*) Do you mean there are difficulties I don't know about, which mean we can't count on Giovanni's support any longer?

LUISA: Giovanni, in a way, has . . . a different problem to solve.

TOMASO: What is it?

LUISA: Our son.

TOMASO: Is he not well?

LUISA: No.

TOMASO: Is he here?

LUISA: No. He's dead.

TOMASO: Ah, yes. Please forgive me. I remember now.

LUISA: Of course, even at the time we kept it hushed up.

TOMASO: But it was years ago.

LUISA: Yes.

TOMASO: And what is the difficulty, exactly?

LUISA: We still haven't managed to come to any . . . agreement.

TOMASO: About what?

LUISA: The accident.

TOMASO: (*cautiously*) Ah, yes, it was an accident. I don't remember it very clearly.

LUISA: He'd be nearly twenty now. You think Giovanni's wrong to stay up here like this, I suppose?

TOMASO: Indeed I do.

LUISA: Guido—our boy was called Guido: one doesn't know whether to say *was* called or *is* called, in cases like that, does one?—Guido loved being up here. When he was small he used to build little houses. His hands . . . they were always touching things . . . it's as if the places were still warm where his hands had been. Here, for example . . . and here. My husband is a great man, isn't he?

TOMASO: Why, yes.

LUISA: I've always loved him and admired him enormously. And Guido, of course, idolised him. What I meant was that my husband always likes to be able to reason things out; he has a logical mind, and it distresses him not to be able to find an explanation.

TOMASO: Explanation of what?

LUISA: The accident. And naturally it does all seem very strange that a young boy . . . he was so *alive*, you see, and good-looking; he had dark brown hair and a nice clear skin; he was fifteen and very, very intelligent . . . it's so shocking that in the space of a second all that should . . . finish. And just by chance: accident. Without a reason; with nothing you can catch on to. It's natural that anyone with a logical mind should feel uneasy, and keep on searching, isn't it?

TOMASO: Yes, naturally.

LUISA: But searching for what? Hundreds of accidents happen; and there's no reason for any of them.

TOMASO: And is that why you think Giovanni . . .?

LUISA: Yes. Perhaps it's partly on my account as well . . . Though really I ought to . . . My husband takes such care of me, even more than he did before. I couldn't live without him. (GIOVANNI's *footsteps are heard; she drops her voice.*) I really don't think you'll find him any use to you now. (*She moves towards the stairs, and pauses there.*)

GIOVANNI: (*comes in without seeing his wife; he looks at* TOMASO, *smiling.*) I see you've brought Raniero with you; he's just coming up. And a lot of others as well. What's the matter? Are you holding a party conference up here? I'm beginning to feel quite flattered . . .

He follows TOMASO's *glance, and sees* LUISA. *She smiles, and goes away upstairs.*

GIOVANNI: (*turning to* TOMASO, *and resuming*) I'm beginning to feel quite flattered, if all this is for *my* benefit. (*A brief pause.*) Has my wife been talking to you?

TOMASO: Yes.

GIOVANNI: She told you?

TOMASO: Yes.

GIOVANNI: She still hasn't got over the shock, I'm afraid.

TOMASO: Was he the only child?

GIOVANNI: Yes.

TOMASO: (*carefully feeling his way*) I suppose I must have seen him.

GIOVANNI: Probably. At all my public speeches there was always a little boy sitting on a chair behind me, very self-possessed.

TOMASO: Ah, that was he?

GIOVANNI: Yes, that was Guido. Fine impression of his father he must have got. Forgive me for asking, but what did Luisa tell you?

TOMASO: Well, you can imagine . . .

GIOVANNI: (*after a pause*) The trouble is that my wife saw the boy after.

TOMASO: Was he . . .?

GIOVANNI: Yes, rather smashed up.

TOMASO: Was he run over?

GIOVANNI: (*absently*) M'm? Yes, yes. Just like that, suddenly.

TOMASO: (*cautiously*) It's happening the whole time. There's so much traffic.

GIOVANNI: Yes. Wheels. Such a quick, complete destruction of a human being . . .

TOMASO: I suppose it's chiefly your wife who . . .?

GIOVANNI: . . . keeps on thinking about it. Yes.

TOMASO: What is it that . . . worries her particularly?

GIOVANNI: (*is silent for a moment.*) At first she didn't want them to take him away. Then, after a time she stopped talking about it. And then, later on, one night, we were sitting quietly reading in front of the fire . . . and she looked up . . . and asked me a question.

TOMASO: About what had happened?

GIOVANNI: Yes. I replied. And ever since then, every so often, we go over it all again. Luisa has dug up thousands of small details about it, thousands of them.

TOMASO: For what purpose?

LUISA: (*who, a few moments ago, has reappeared on the stairs*) To try and understand; to try and work it all out. Poor Giovanni, I torment him the whole time. Giovanni, why did you say he'd been run over?

GIOVANNI: Oh, nothing. It seemed simpler, that's all. (*To* TOMASO) It comes to the same thing. Most accidents are street accidents, after all.

LUISA: Our son fell from the window of our flat. We'd been out for the evening.

GIOVANNI: He said he'd rather stay at home, and read.

LUISA: Excuse me, Giovanni, he never said what book it was, did he?

GIOVANNI: (*gently*) I've told you before, dear, it's one of the points I can't recall.

LUISA: Poor Giovanni.

GIOVANNI: No, no, my dear, it's only natural that you should want to know.

LUISA: (*to* TOMASO) You see, the book was actually found afterwards, lying there open. Unfortunately people rushed in almost at once, handling everything, moving things about. ...

GIOVANNI: They upset the place rather.

LUISA: Yes. What happened was ... when we got home that night, we found ...

GIOVANNI: My dear, I really don't think Tomaso can be interested in all this ...

LUISA: But perhaps Tomaso can give us his views as well; he can tell us what *he* thinks about it. (*To* TOMASO) You see: we came back that night——

GIOVANNI: (*continuing with his eyes on the ground, as though re-reading the same page for the twentieth time*) ... and went in. Luisa found the bed empty. She looked everywhere in the flat. He wasn't there. Then I heard Luisa open the door on the staircase and run downstairs. I called out after her: "Luisa: Luisa, what's the matter?"

(*With a change of voice*) Luisa, what did you think? Why did you run? (LUISA *does not reply.*) And when I got down there . . . (*He ends with a conclusive gesture.*)

LUISA: Tell him everything.

GIOVANNI: In the courtyard, there was a flower-bed . . . full of weeds. No one had bothered to look after it for a long time. Luisa had got there before me; she was standing there in the dark, looking down at something in the flower-bed. (*A silence.*)

LUISA: (*to* TOMASO) We'd locked the door of the flat before going out, you see. That's the point. That's the reason we can't stop thinking about it. The door of the flat. (*To* GIOVANNI) Tell him.

GIOVANNI: Yes. (*Reciting as before*) Yes. When we left Guido, and went out, I . . .

LUISA: Or perhaps it was I . . .

GIOVANNI: No, no, you know it wasn't you. It was me I turned the key in the lock of the front door of the flat. There was nothing out of the ordinary in that. It was instinctive, force of habit.

LUISA: Yes, of course, of course.

GIOVANNI: Nothing anyone could be blamed for. I've always been a very orderly person. It may even have been an impulse of protectiveness, knowing that Guido was going to stay in the flat alone.

LUISA: (*prompting him*) Tell him about the window.

GIOVANNI: Yes. When we went out, I also closed the window on the landing outside the front door. It was me again. Without thinking. So that it shouldn't bang if there was a wind.

LUISA: (*with lowered gaze*) Unfortunately, Guido . . . The cigarettes!

GIOVANNI: He hadn't any cigarettes. There were no cigarettes found either in Guido's pockets or in the flat.

LUISA: He liked to smoke. He couldn't bear to be without a cigarette.

GIOVANNI: And so I'm afraid he was ... rather careless. He wanted to go out and buy some.

LUISA: And when he found the front door was locked ...

GIOVANNI: He got out of one of the windows of the flat, and tried to get along a ledge outside it as far as the window on the landing ...

LUISA: But that window was also ...

GIOVANNI: Yes, he found that was locked too. So he had to go back. Half-way back, on the ledge, we found the mark ... the trace ... where he lost his footing.

LUISA: (*fixedly*) The shout.

GIOVANNI: (*gently*) We asked, later, if anyone had heard ... the shout.

LUISA: Someone had, but hadn't taken any notice.

GIOVANNI: (*half-smiling to* TOMASO) The fact is that it would be something of a relief for Luisa—and for me as well—to find there was even the slightest trace of responsibility on the part of someone or something. It would all seem to be much more natural, wouldn't it?

At the outer doors a man has appeared unobserved; a little behind him, a girl. TOMASO *alone has seen them, he makes a sign to them to stay where they are.*

GIOVANNI: But there is no responsibility, none at all ... (*He smiles.*) I might almost say: unfortunately. That's how it is, my dear. (*With an impatient shudder*) Like that. (*Gently again*) Like that.

LUISA: Yes. Giovanni's always so convincing. It gives me immense reassurance, just to hear him. (*She retreats to the stairs; then turns to* TOMASO.) The trouble is that I (*with a smile*) keep play-acting in my head the whole time. It's my hobby; I can't help it. When I've nothing to do I pass the time imagining . . . (*She is silent for a moment, thinking.*) . . . that none of it ever happened. It would have needed so little: if the door hadn't been locked, or even if the window had been open. And Guido going through the rooms like that, humming . . . he always hummed the same tune. (*She murmurs the tune already heard.*) And then everything's all right. And Guido's grown up. He isn't here, of course, but that's because he's away at the University and can't leave. Or perhaps he's got engaged and is frightened to come and tell us. Or he may have been held up at the frontier. I enjoy pretending. And after all a lot of people do the same: they imagine things in the greatest detail . . . But I actually *say* them, and then Giovanni scolds me. I talk to Giovanni as if Guido were actually on his way here; it's play-acting. Perhaps it is a little morbid, but I'm perfectly conscious of what I'm doing. Poor Giovanni. (*Suddenly*) For example, I say to him: (*With complete naturalness*) But, Giovanni, why hasn't he written to us this week?

GIOVANNI: (*with persuasive quietness*) Luisa, you know quite well that Guido can't ever write to us again.

LUISA: Oh, I know, but do you think they'll let him through quickly, up at the frontier?

GIOVANNI: Guido isn't held up at the frontier: you know he isn't. He's dead, poor boy.

LUISA: I know, I know. (*To* TOMASO, *pointing*) That

isn't Guido calling from the pass up there. (*A murmur of wind has been heard.*)

GIOVANNI: It isn't good for you, Luisa, to persist in these games of make-believe.

LUISA: (*to* TOMASO) But it's perfectly harmless, isn't it? Because I know perfectly well it's only a waste of time. (*With a smile*) Oh, Giovanni, I do hope you won't send me to the lunatic asylum.

GIOVANNI: My dear, you mustn't say that, even in fun.

LUISA: I'm sorry.

GIOVANNI: And if it really is only a waste of time, I think you ought to give it up.

LUISA: Yes. (*She moves away towards the stairs; then turns back again.*) Giovanni, do you know something I've discovered? I've never told you before. I've discovered that it isn't quite only a waste of time. (*Pause.*) The reason is: that I sometimes have a feeling of guilt.

A certain agitation seems to enter the room. Perhaps it is only the murmur of the wind.

GIOVANNI: Guilt? Whatever for? We've gone over it a thousand times . . .

LUISA: No, no, not because of what happened. But before. Guido's life was so short. (*To* TOMASO) And now, when I think back over it, I have the feeling that in that short time we never somehow . . . made him as happy as we should have.

GIOVANNI: (*indignantly*) But, please, my dear, that's absurd. Have you any grounds for thinking so?

LUISA: No, no. It simply occurred to me.

GIOVANNI: (*still indignant*) But I tell you it was just the opposite. I can't think any boy in the world was ever looked after as Guido was. Too much so, perhaps. Isn't that so?

LUISA: Yes, of course it is.

GIOVANNI: Why, Tomaso, he was idolised, safeguarded, cared for, protected . . . He wanted for nothing a boy of fifteen could possibly wish for . . . (*To* LUISA) Did he?

LUISA: No, no.

GIOVANNI: He was always with us, wherever we went. It was he himself who didn't want to go out that evening.

LUISA: Yes, it's quite true.

GIOVANNI: (*gradually regaining his control and quietness*) Why, I've even sometimes thought we actually spoiled him. Luisa, do you realise what the truth of the matter is? Our own thoughts always create scruples of conscience and feelings of guilt about the dead—out of nothing. We imagine they've looked at us in such and such a way, or that there was something we ought to have said . . .

LUISA: Yes, but what?

GIOVANNI: Exactly: it's all an illusion. Perhaps you think I was a bit too severe with him?

LUISA: No, no: just the opposite.

GIOVANNI: I never took my eyes off him. And perhaps it's true that the glance of those who love us does weigh on us a little, does bind us. But it does also comfort and encourage us sometimes, perhaps.

LUISA: Yes, of course.

GIOVANNI: We did absolutely everything we could for him, Tomaso. Naturally as the boy grew up he became more reserved. He wasn't so noisy or child-like. But that's so with all children, it's the great thing about growing up.

LUISA: Yes, of course. It would really be best if he himself came and explained it all to us, but they've held him up at the pass.

GIOVANNI: In any case, he was a cheerful boy. I know he was educated and precocious, and aware of everything that went on; but he was cheerful. He was happy.

LUISA: Yes, yes. Perhaps, that last night, if I'd only . . . oh, if I'd only known . . . (*Her voice breaks.*) I could have been more open, I could have . . . held him close to me, close, close . . . (*As she withdraws, sobbing*) I could have covered him with tenderness, hugged him tight to me . . . And instead, I always held back because I was ashamed to. . . . (*She has gone.*)

The daylight is fading; there is still light on the distant peaks.

GIOVANNI: (*his voice is under control again; he wipes a little moisture from his hands.*) Yes, one's ashamed to show how fond one is . . . or to feel oneself loved too much. And perhaps Guido himself . . . (*Repeats*) Guido. (*With a sudden mild exasperation*) Guido. (*Quietly again*) Guido. (*To the others*) Please forgive me. Ah, hello, Raniero, you've come too. Well, my dear friends, perhaps it's as well you've heard all this. At least you'll have seen what complex reasons I have at the moment for being . . . glad, yes, doubly glad, at the thought of a change, the thought of coming back to . . . to my old job, my old work, with you. Though not just at once, of course, not just yet.

TOMASO: Why not yet?

GIOVANNI: Not just yet.

TOMASO: (*signs to* RANIERO *to come in; and, sitting down, says*) Is there some connection we don't quite understand between our political problems and the loss of your son?

GIOVANNI: M'm? No. Good heavens, no. How should there be?

TOMASO: I only wanted to be sure. Just to try and get things straight. Unfortunately, once things are over there's nothing one can do about them. Digging them up again doesn't help. The world goes round and round, all by itself, as a matter of course.

GIOVANNI: (*after a brief pause*) Yes, indubitably. And as I say, I do intend to take up my old contacts with you the minute I'm able. Yes. I'll let you know. God knows, it's my duty to. We're agreed about most things after all.... (*Pause.*) Look: if you want to get back to the village before dark, you really ought to start out at once. (*A silence.*)

RANIERO: (*gently*) No, Giovanni. We didn't come with the intention of going back immediately.

GIOVANNI *looks at* TOMASO.

TOMASO: Yes, there is something we have to do first. Here. (*He hesitates a moment.*) Giovanni: I want you to listen carefully and seriously to what I'm going to say to you. Sit down.

GIOVANNI *does so.*

TOMASO: (*with great simplicity*) It's quite clear, Giovanni, that you've become a little over-absorbed in your own personal problems. But the world has gone on, just the same. What were we saying a little while ago? Half a mile from here is the point of attrition between two great wheels. Two black, heavy clouds, waiting for the first thunderbolt. That's why we're here; it's almost a question of hours; we came in a great hurry. The Advisory Council is meeting the day after tomorrow; everybody's very anxious. They'll either decide on postponement, which is perhaps the worst decision of all, since it means eternal attrition; slow destruction. Or else a clean break: conflict. Quite a number of people are hoping for that; even catastrophe has its uses; and its supporters too. Or else . . .

RANIERO: An agreement.

TOMASO: An agreement. (*Brief pause.*) A number of people, both on our side of the frontier and theirs, have had the idea of forcing the hands of both governments—forcing them in the good sense, I mean—while there's still time. It means going right over the heads of the official powers, who in fact, at this stage, must be kept unaware of what's going on. So, as you see, our preparations are in the nature of a conspiracy. That's what I'm here to explain to you. It's been agreed that the move shall be made simultaneously by two groups of "big" men, one lot from our side, one from theirs.

RANIERO *rises and switches on a light.*

TOMASO: They will move towards each other across those fields out there. The setting is very imposing: it'll stir people's imagination. A number of newspapermen, who are already here, will observe from a distance. The two groups will approach each other, shake hands, take from their pockets their admirable lists of proposals, and fix the basis for an understanding. There are some people who think that pacification simply means postponing the war; I don't agree with them. Within an hour the news will have gone round the world: it's hoped it will make both governments give in; and they don't, as a matter of fact, ask anything better. It's an honest attempt. If it succeeds, well, then, there may be peace. If it doesn't, then things will be simply as they were before. Though possibly we ourselves shall get into trouble. I'm very sorry I haven't the leisure to explain things more thoroughly.

GIOVANNI: Are the proposals already decided on?

TOMASO: They can always be reconsidered.

GIOVANNI: What is in them?

TOMASO: Just general suggestions for an agreement about principles.

GIOVANNI: (*reflects*) But however can we come to an agreement with error?

TOMASO: Perhaps "error" isn't entirely on their side.

GIOVANNI: I'm just trying to think what the catch is.

TOMASO: There's no catch; that would be unthinkable. It's a meeting. The other side want it too.

GIOVANNI: What about the guards? Won't they shoot?

TOMASO: We have friends who have seen to that.

GIOVANNI: And the meeting's to be up there?

TOMASO: Yes. Any point of the frontier would have done. But we're better defended here against possible leakages. Besides, *you* live here.

GIOVANNI: Me? Why me?

TOMASO: You'll be with us. The occasion will bear your name.

GIOVANNI: It's a surprising honour, I must say.

TOMASO: You're the only one of us with a legend to your name. We had to have someone who really counted.

GIOVANNI: When is it to be?

TOMASO: Tomorrow. It's the latest possible day.

GIOVANNI: And you've left it as late as this, before coming here?

TOMASO: We had to prevent counter-measures.

GIOVANNI: And this extraordinary way of coming up here to get me? And only deciding on me at the last moment? A bit offensive, isn't it, I'd have thought?

TOMASO: We didn't originally choose you, as a matter of fact. It's rather amusing really, the way these things work out by themselves. The whole thing never originally concerned you. We originally picked on the man who supplanted you: (*lightly*) your dear old enemy Nicola.

RANIERO: Nicola's very ill; he can't last much longer.

TOMASO: No. He's out of the question; it would kill him. We kept hoping, right up to yesterday. And then we saw it had to be you. It's much more important than your personal problems, Giovanni. Children die, and the world still goes on. (*With vague nonchalance he points, as though towards some distant panorama.*) The world. People are muttering and haggling in every corner. But in reality they're all moving on. You must put yourself at their head, and lead them forward, so that they'll all of them be happier, as far as is humanly possible. You must wake up, Giovanni.

GIOVANNI: Wouldn't it all be the same without me?

TOMASO: (*still amiably*) No. Everything's arranged. We came to you at the last moment. Besides, there's your wife to consider: she'd be very glad to close this painful chapter of your lives, I'm sure.

GIOVANNI: I only meant ... are you sure this business is really anything to do with me?

TOMASO: (*humbly and simply*) Listen: a people's leader is a man who works very close to a lamp. He himself is quite small. But his shadow is a long one. Consequences, responsibilities: you can't simply leave those behind as you can leave a hotel bedroom. Five years ought to be enough rest for anybody, however tired they are. The account's falling due. You asked a good deal in the old days; you were very exacting. It's only fair you should pay the price.

GIOVANNI: I never assumed any obligations. It was the rest of you who did that. I was outside it all.

TOMASO *reflects for a moment, rises, and beckons to the girl who has till now remained outside on the threshold. She enters; she is beautiful and very young and wears large glasses.* RANIERO *switches on another light.*

TOMASO: Rosa, my dear, I'm afraid I shall have to ask your patient to come in here. Would you be kind enough to go and fetch him? ... Oh, just a moment. (*He points to* GIOVANNI.) Do you recognise who this is?

ROSA: Of course. Everyone remembers him with immense gratitude.

TOMASO: But he doesn't know who you are. (*To* GIOVANNI) This charming girl is an orphan; the revolution has adopted her. She is our flower. We owe *her* a debt of gratitude too. It's possible we should never have won, if it hadn't been for ... (*To* ROSA) But suppose you tell him, my dear.

ROSA: He means if it hadn't been for the sacrifice of my father. My father was a very good and respected man. He was always called the Baker.

TOMASO: Go on.

ROSA: He was in the Square, with the crowd that marched to the ex-Ministry, on the sixth of July. There was a shot. My father fell. That's the kind of thing that doesn't happen now. Our enemies had killed him, in cold blood. But his death proved of great value. It was the spark. Everyone loved him so much, though he was only a humble workman. (*In a low voice*) I hope to do things that would have made him proud of me. (*A silence.*)

GIOVANNI: (*has lowered his gaze*) Are you the daughter of Andrea the Baker?

ROSA: Yes.

GIOVANNI: And what are your feelings towards the men who killed your father?

ROSA: I've forgiven them. I never wanted to hate them. (*She turns and goes out.*)

TOMASO: (*following her with his eyes*) Innocent, loyal angel! She's a nurse. I wonder what she'd feel, if she knew . . .

GIOVANNI: They were not my orders.

TOMASO: . . . if she knew that shot wasn't fired by the others, but by us. We had to have a dead man. Anybody, so long as he was dead; there, in the Square. So that the scales would tip up. And it happened to be Andrea the Baker.

GIOVANNI: It was not I who gave the order.

RANIERO: Giovanni, you're not being quite honest now.

TOMASO: You concerned yourself only with general principles: as is the way with apostles. You said what you needed was an incident. The words were pure and clean; it was the facts that were covered with blood.

RANIERO: (*amiably, as he walks to the back*) It's all very well sitting down to a well-cooked dinner, pretending not to know what goes on in the kitchen. (*He goes out.*)

TOMASO: In any case one man's life is a small price. The chariot has to pass. It was an excellent decision; we had to make many of them: I, you, Raniero; and Nicola. If we're still here, part of the credit for it is due to you. In a few moments Nicola will be here as well.

GIOVANNI: Nicola? I thought you said he was ill?

TOMASO: He's come at the risk of his life.

GIOVANNI: Andrea dead, Nicola dying. Strange reunion.

TOMASO: It's the Executive that's meeting; it is deliberating in emergency conditions. It rules Nicola out as unfitted, at the suggestion of, and with the vote of, Nicola himself. It elects you in his place. It nominates the Rendezvous Committee for tomorrow: Raniero and myself, with you as chairman. We have the whole night before us. (*Looking towards the door*) Ah, here's Nicola.

A group of people is entering; a middle-aged man, NICOLA, *whose walk and bearing make him seem older than he is: he is supported by a stranger on one side, on the other side by* ROSA. RANIERO *is just behind them.*

ROSA: (*helping* NICOLA *down a step*) Come along. Don't be afraid.

NICOLA: (*docilely*) Yes, yes. (*He stands, breathing heavily, looking at* TOMASO *and* GIOVANNI.) I feel much better.

ROSA: Sit down. (*She makes him sit down, with the assistance of the stranger, who immediately afterwards goes out.*)

NICOLA: (*to* ROSA) What a long time you left me by myself.

ROSA: It wasn't my fault. (*Proudly, to the others*) He won't even eat, if I'm not there. (*To* NICOLA) I wonder however you got on before? And how you'll get on when you're better, and start looking after yourself.

GIOVANNI: Hello, Nicola. Not well?

NICOLA: It's the heart: a bit of a breakdown. The doctor says I'm improving. I'm here on your account. I expect they've told you. I'm everybody's friend now. I'm not your enemy any more ... or anybody else's. In any case, I always admired you. This is Rosa: she's my martyr, she's my sweetheart. Rosa the adorable, Rosa most precious, Rosa most virtuous ... My little healer, my real doctor.

ROSA: You mustn't talk so much.

TOMASO: You can leave him now, Rosa.

NICOLA: If there's no objection ... I'd rather like her to stay. She won't be any trouble. She could stay just outside the door. She won't hear anything. You couldn't find anyone safer than Rosa.

ROSA: (*stepping forward*) Mr. Nicola always feels much happier when I'm here.

TOMASO *regards* NICOLA *in silence.*

NICOLA: (*after a pause*) No, it's impossible, Rosa. Go along. We are holding a meeting. It won't last long. I'm all right. Don't go too far away.

TOMASO: (*to* ROSA) I'll call you back myself. (*To* LUISA, *who has reappeared*) I must ask you also to leave us, madam. We're obliged to be rather strict about this, I'm afraid. It won't take long.

ROSA: (*goes in silence to the door, then turns.*) I'd like to say before I go that ... (*Re-approaching*) Mr. Tomaso, and Mr. Giovanni, I feel it's my duty to ... there's something I ought to ...

NICOLA: (*harshly*) Now you're being awkward, my dear. You're trying any excuse in order to stay. Go along with you. I'm feeling very well indeed. Go on.

A silence. ROSA *goes out and disappears in the background.* LUISA *withdraws.* TOMASO *watches both women out of sight, and then sits.*

TOMASO: The meeting is open.

They all sit.

NICOLA: (*to* GIOVANNI) You must be pleased? You've always been lucky. I have to give up my place to you. A little sickness ten days ago. I'd been overworking ... I never realised I was working for you. They all swear I'd never be able to get up there. Ah, well ... you're the most suitable man for the job. I'm in complete agreement with Tomaso; about everything. The honour will be yours.

GIOVANNI: (*rising*) I have a statement to make. You must not think it is simply fatigue that obliges me to ... to decline this undertaking. The real reason is that my ideas have changed. (*Brief pause*) I believe that all this time we have been making a mistake.

A silence.

TOMASO: (*quietly*) Well? We are listening.

CURTAIN

ACT TWO

It is night, and stars are shining over the mountains. TOMASO, RANIERO *and* NICOLA, *seated, are listening to* GIOVANNI.

GIOVANNI: (*laughing nervously*) And why have my ideas changed? Well, they've changed, that's all. It's not easy to explain why. There are various reasons. For example, this very question of making speeches. Speeches were making me ill.

RANIERO: What do you mean?

GIOVANNI: They were upsetting me. I listened to too many, of course: other people's, and my own: recorded. It's highly instructive. Was I, or wasn't I, a leader of the people? The life of a leader etcetera is a life of making speeches. Lofty ideas. (*Half to himself*) My mouth used to get so dry. And then again, all those gestures . . . (*He imitates an orator's gestures.*) My arms used to ache. (*He laughs.*) Friends, friends, I'm only joking. We all know every public speech is a piece of acting. I wonder what Guido used to make of it all; children can be very critical. I always dragged him after me; I used to think I might one day use him, make him my successor. And he always wanted to hear me, too . . . (*Pause. Then he laughs again, and touches his ear.*) But most of all, the trouble was . . . the auditory disturbances: always hearing the same tune: Tatá-tatáta . . . tatá-tatáta . . . Solemn. But something more than solemn: tormented; embittered. Tatá-tatáta. Tatá-tatáta . . . Why! Whatever's the matter with that poor gentleman? (*Answering*) Nothing, no, no, the man's quite happy. It's the voice. The voice for collective use is always angry. Sinister. With a friend it's possible to talk. With a thousand, God knows why, something comes up from the depths, from underground; something funereal, almost prophetic . . . tatá-tatáta . . . (*He laughs.*) Auditory disturbances.

RANIERO: Giovanni.

GIOVANNI: Oh, yes, I know, I'm not being serious. Disgraceful of me, considering the circumstances. But what about the faces? I couldn't bear all the faces, either. Oh, nor could you, I know. The thing that prompts a leader of the people to try and change the people is that the people as they are disgust him. Ugly faces, wherever you go. And the words I spoke: people absorbed them, or otherwise, precisely according to the amount of venom they contained. Humus: that's what they found there. A reserve of bad temper in suspension. Spite; spite; everywhere. (*He laughs.*) Ah, my dear friends, just go for a little walk some time: and look at them, look at the people. If they bump into one another, they turn and swear. (*He laughs.*) Full of bile. The breath of carnivores. They're full of hate even in their games. My wife: after the accident she didn't want to see me. Let's hope that now . . . But it's the same everywhere: husbands sneering at their wives, children sneering at their parents.

RANIERO: Like yourself at this moment.

GIOVANNI: I speak like my epoch.

RANIERO: You mean all these accusations aren't accusations against us: just against the epoch?

GIOVANNI: But it's *we* who put our signatures to the

epoch. It's an epoch in which everybody has to have some great dislike, which they can tend, like a plant in a pot. (*He laughs.*) It means . . .

RANIERO: What?

GIOVANNI: If you want to rouse people and drag them after you, there's only one way: tell them that where they are at the moment they're unfortunate; downtrodden; wretched. Why? Why, because someone else has been naughty. In order to be happy, we always need some particular object: something not inside us, but out. Something we can pick up and carry away: a parcel. If we haven't got it, it's obviously because somebody's stolen it from us. A parcel: see one in someone else's hands, and it gnaws at your heart. (*He laughs.*) A perpetual gnawing. But you must forgive me: I'm just meandering. What about you? You sit there listening to me like three angels. You almost frighten me.

RANIERO: (*amiably*) We imagine you have other and more serious things to say to us, as well; we merely suppose you're working around to them.

GIOVANNI: Yes, perhaps that's it.

TOMASO: (*lifting his face, which he has been resting against one hand*) In any case, we're following you with the greatest interest, of course.

GIOVANNI: (*astonished*) For God's sake, Tomaso. What's going on?

TOMASO: What's going on is that we've decided to come to terms with our enemies. Why? The reason's obvious: *we also* have ceased to believe our ideas are all right and theirs all wrong.

GIOVANNI: (*sarcastically*) Are you talking seriously?

TOMASO: (*ignoring him*) . . . and we think there's

something to be said for both points of view. We're trying to find the starting-point which may form the basis up there tomorrow, for an understanding ... between us and them.

GIOVANNI: (*almost chanting*) Us and them, us and them! (*He laughs.*) Tomaso, do you know what's worrying me? That "us and them" are really one and the same thing. That's why we quarrel with them: it's really a competition.

RANIERO: (*respectfully*) The same in what way?

GIOVANNI: (*laughs*) The high-ups, the tricks, the methods. They're all so much alike. This side and that, there's always the Cause. The Cause. Sublime trade-mark; balm from heaven.

RANIERO: (*curiously patient*) Go on.

GIOVANNI: Everything's upside down. Killing: it's no longer punishable. That side and this. We've all of us, and I most of all, paid precious little regard to ... (*He breaks off.*)

A stranger enters, goes over to TOMASO, *and whispers to him. After a nod from* TOMASO, *he goes out again.*

GIOVANNI: (*resuming*) We've fixed up a great many frauds. (*Sarcastically*) Decision: oh yes, of course. Hail, men of iron, that's the expression, isn't it? Iron. Tonight I see you all united. Or am I wrong?

RANIERO: We are still waiting to hear what you have to say.

GIOVANNI: What I mean is that the Cause is very exacting; and I'm a little sick of being the one that exacts. If I really had to go up there tomorrow morning to the frontier, the first thing I should propose is that all the high-ups on both sides should be compelled to cat their dress-uniforms cut up in strips. Compelled above everything else, to apologise.

RANIERO: (*still deferentially*) My dear Giovanni, you're still playing with us. What is it you really mean?

GIOVANNI: Perhaps I don't even know myself. I'm acting the fool, and beginning to feel rather ashamed.

RANIERO: And whom do you want us to apologise to?

GIOVANNI: Why, to . . . everyone. The people.

RANIERO: Do you mean we've sometimes acted in our own interests?

GIOVANNI: Oh, no, never. Nor have the others, over there.

RANIERO: Everything we've ever done and thought has been for the people.

GIOVANNI: (*expostulating*) The others are the same. It's the same mistake.

RANIERO: And what is the mistake?

GIOVANNI: You've said yourself. We are philanthropists, and we think too much about other people. On both sides; with different systems. We've decided too many things on other people's behalf. We set out to make people happy. And in consequence, the people have been left with so little to look after for themselves that they've become . . . fed up. (*Pause.*) Besides . . .

RANIERO: Besides what?

GIOVANNI: (*following his own train of thought*) . . . a man's troubles; so long as he has to look after them himself . . . they remain (*shrugs*) just one man's troubles. His own: they look like him.

(*He breaks off for a second.* LUISA *is heard again, offstage, singing.*)

GIOVANNI: (*resuming*) But multiply them by millions and what do they become? They turn into tonnage, and volume. Inevitably. Book-keeping, inspections. Rations, time-tables.

RANIERO: So that's the mistake, is it?

GIOVANNI: And why is it a mistake? It's sacrosanct. Organisation always *is* sacrosanct. (*Pause.*) But what do we do about human follies? (*With a growing, inexplicable exasperation*) We take little account of folly. As if it didn't exist. But it does.

RANIERO: How do you mean?

GIOVANNI: I mean that men are full of whims and fancies. Heaven help them if they had to describe them to anyone. Think of those millions and millions of blades of grass out there, not one of them exactly like another, each aspiring to God knows what, differing, erring. Variations. Perhaps it's only by some mistake that things *do* differ from each other. And perhaps the distinctive human product is folly, and man is only a garden for its cultivation. Sheep can have offspring, as we can; horses can draw carts as we can; but *folly*—only man is capable of that. It would be a great joke if it turned out that the reallest things weren't a matter of statistics at all and the world were . . . an immense tree of follies; growing, growing, every leaf another folly, each one more extraordinary than the last, on and up, and on the topmost branch one folly above all . . . that really took one's breath away! And if all this were essential to man? His element, like water to the fish? We ought to have paid much more respect to folly.

RANIERO: Perhaps we were otherwise engaged. What

we've tried to do isn't the kind of thing to be cast aside lightly; security, well-being ...

GIOVANNI: Standard of living ...

RANIERO: Beyond those, I don't know what you think the duties of a government ought to be.

TOMASO: (*lifting his face from his hand for a moment*) Or of a father. Like yours towards your son, for example.

RANIERO: People have rather strange tastes, they want to be fed, and clothed, warmed, housed ...

GIOVANNI: ... disinfected ...

RANIERO: It's easy for the well fed to sneer at such things.

GIOVANNI: And quite wrong, too. I'm like a tiger if the stove over there won't draw. Heating; ventilation; order, production, reproduction, hygiene. There's only one trouble with it all.

RANIERO: Perhaps you'll be good enough to tell us what it is?

GIOVANNI: (*looks at him for a moment, shrugs his shoulders and says, in protest*) ... Well, aren't all these things more like the business of a stock-breeder? Haven't we all become rather too zootechnical?

RANIERO: Is that all?

GIOVANNI: Our standards are those of a vet. We think they're the only positive standards there are. It's an idea that's got about, a sort of contagion.

RANIERO: Well, what of it?

GIOVANNI: Men are still vain enough to feel uneasy. They're not wholly satisfied with the thought that all that progress means is merely dying fatter, cleaner, better dressed.

RANIERO: Have you a better solution to offer?

GIOVANNI: No, but everyone's all become rather discouraged by the whole thing. Have you ever noticed the look in the eyes of oxen on the country roads? Sad. *Bos. Pecus.* They're not sure they matter any longer. Over there and over here. They know something's missing.

RANIERO: What?

GIOVANNI: (*shrugs*) I don't know either. But it ... (*almost to himself*) it's like an illness. There's a kind of epidemic in the world. When people are all together, they don't notice it. Crowded squares, crowded football-grounds, everyone happy. Then they go back home. And once again all of them have that look in their eyes. Sad. *Bos. Pecus.* They don't know what to do. They go from one room to another, whistling. Don't leave them alone. They feel ... stupefied when they are alone. They go and look at themselves in the mirror, they stare at their own expression. They don't believe it; they don't believe they're real. Don't leave them alone.

TOMASO: (*again raising his head*) Does your disillusionment come from some personal cause, by any chance?

GIOVANNI: No. Why should it?

TOMASO: I'm sorry, I was still thinking of the death of your son.

GIOVANNI: (*angrily*) What has my son to do with it?

TOMASO: (*politely*) It was your wife who made the suggestion: that in his brief span of life your son hadn't been altogether happy. And I wouldn't like you to lay any of the blame for that on us.

GIOVANNI: No! I've told you so already. That's quite another matter.

TOMASO: Your uneasiness about him ...

GIOVANNI: Uneasiness! What do you mean: uneasiness? What uneasiness? (*Controlling himself*) My son was a happy boy. He has nothing to do with all this. The problem of my son is simply the fact of a door: a door, locked absent-mindedly. (*He thinks for a moment: then shrugs his shoulders.*) In any case I'm the last to attach any importance to my own chatter. I'm just talking for the talking's sake.

TOMASO: (*rising*) And unfortunately time is getting on. Our action is in the executive stage. We can't postpone it for the pleasures of discussion, however valuable. The arrangements have already been completed by ourselves . . . (*turning suddenly to* NICOLA) and Nicola. We too, together with Nicola, have recognised some of our errors. This new move of ours is, in fact, aimed at remedying them. It's a move we and Nicola have decided to make. Whatever happens. Tomorrow.

NICOLA: (*also rising*) And I unfortunately am sick. I beg your pardon very sincerely. It's not just a figure of speech; I'm sick. (*His words are spoken calmly, but it is obvious that he is controlling himself only with difficulty.*) If there'd been the slightest chance . . . I wouldn't have foregone it. But there was no alternative. Let me make myself clear: I refuse, yes, I refuse to force you to carry a corpse up there with you. Or to leave one behind you half way there. It would be embarrassing. It would make the worst possible impression. (*Suddenly shouting*) There are duties in life, my dear Giovanni, there are duties . . . !

TOMASO: No, please, Nicola, please. You mustn't get excited.

NICOLA: I never thought that all our efforts could

be ... jeopardised at the last moment. I know I'm upset ... but it's not just ... because of my own life; that ... that matters less than nothing; and it's quite right that ...

TOMASO: (*calmly, to* GIOVANNI) His condition really is quite serious. (*Dropping his voice*) Touch and go, I would say. I'm sorry, Nicola, but this is not the time for idle courtesies. What's knocked you out we all understand. But you must control yourself, or try to.

NICOLA: Yes, of course, I know. (*Nevertheless his voice quickly becomes agitated again.*) But I refuse, I tell you, I categorically refuse ... to countenance such a misunderstanding! I intend ... to denounce it, to speak out! The world shall know ... the truth. There are newspapermen out there in that field. (*Hysterically*) It's your duty, my dear Giovanni. You claim to be so pure, so philanthropic. It's up to you. Your son, your son; your successor. If he were here now, you'd be looking very fine, wouldn't you?

TOMASO: (*coldly*) That'll do, Nicola, there's no call for that. (*Amiably*) I am sure that Giovanni will join us. (*Short pause.*) His objections can scarcely excuse him, seeing that we too ... (*turning to* GIOVANNI) we're taking you at your word. I mean that we do, in substance, adopt your point of view. Yes. Perhaps that surprises you. All the same, you might as well know that your ideas, precisely because of their very vagueness, offer us just the opportunity we were looking for: the chance to help us to put this meeting on a high plane from the very start, so that we can disregard our minor disagreements and begin straightway on a level where ... every decent man and woman, on our side and theirs, can't help but be in agreement. Your own opinions——

GIOVANNI: You accept them?

TOMASO: Yes. We accept them. After all, they've never done anyone any harm. You shall formulate the points yourself. You shall say whatever you like; it's a splendid opportunity for you.

He nods to RANIERO. RANIERO *goes out.*

TOMASO: We have, in fact, brought a number of well-disposed newspapermen up here with us. You shall talk to them yourself.

GIOVANNI: Very well.

TOMASO: It's quite true: the world must know. We accept your ideas. It's not a question of pressing on to an agreement at the moment, but simply of paving the way. And after all, your opinions do in fact add dignity to this gesture of ours. We ought almost to be glad Nicola's so ill.

GIOVANNI: Can I talk to him for a few minutes? Nicola, I mean.

TOMASO: (*looks at him, and then at* NICOLA) . . . Yes, that might be a good idea. Nicola is, in a way, handing things over to you. (*To* NICOLA) He's taking your place, Nicola. (*Pause.*) Don't tire yourself out.

NICOLA: No.

TOMASO: (*on his way out, pointing to a side door*) In there, did you say we could receive the newspapermen?

GIOVANNI: Yes.

TOMASO: Good. (*He goes out at the back.*)

GIOVANNI *and* NICOLA *look at one another.*

NICOLA: Forgive me.

GIOVANNI: What for?

NICOLA: The things I said.

GIOVANNI: Oh, I understand. Your heart, is it?

NICOLA: Yes.

GIOVANNI: When was it?

NICOLA: A few days ago.

GIOVANNI: How?

NICOLA: One of the strings of the instrument snapping, that's all.

GIOVANNI: You were already arranging this business?

NICOLA: Yes. Perhaps it was the excitement.

GIOVANNI: What did they tell you?

NICOLA: That I haven't got much longer, that's all. Days. The doctors were quite definite.

GIOVANNI: Has Tomaso had you looked after?

NICOLA: Yes, he's seen to everything. It is just possible I . . . may pull through.

GIOVANNI: However does Tomaso come to be so accommodating?

NICOLA: With whom?

GIOVANNI: Me.

NICOLA: I don't know. (*A silence.*)

GIOVANNI: Nicola, is there something I don't know about?

NICOLA: (*stares at him*) No. Giovanni, what do you think I hold sacred, or dear in the world? I've never believed in the soul. Though in these days I do find myself thinking a lot about such things. But I swear to you, I swear, I swear, by whatever we are, by whatever it is, life, survival after death, I swear I'm keeping nothing from you. Everything is as I've told you. (*The minute he has finished speaking, he drops his head.*)

GIOVANNI: It's you who ought to forgive me.

NICOLA: (*still looking down, whispers*) My trouble is something else.

GIOVANNI: What?

NICOLA: Do you think I can't see myself? A revolting, monstrous, indecent spectacle. Why don't you all spit all over me?

GIOVANNI: Why should we?

NICOLA: (*with complete simplicity*) I'm afraid of dying; that's what it comes to. Ever since I knew and was sure, quite calmly sure of it—ever since then, I've been just a little heap of guts, dying. I can't stand up straight any more. I didn't believe it myself. No one does to begin with. The mistake's been thinking about it . . . thinking . . . thinking . . . (*Candidly*) I'm frightened, Giovanni. Frightened, that's all. (*Smiling wanly, and breathing heavily*) There's nothing left to me now. My darling Rosa tells me that she's my mother . . . and I'm her baby. (*His teeth chatter.*) I'd really like . . . just to be a baby and know nothing else. (*As to himself*) I'd like to . . . stay alive: even if I was only a paralysed lump: but alive. And now . . . a mistake over an injection would be enough. To live: the idea always seems so tremendous. No-one realises it. Glory, heaven: they're all illusions. You're nothing any more! (*Burying his face in his hands*) I've gone on thinking and thinking and thinking about it.

GIOVANNI: (*pondering*) Does it mean so much, then: to live?

NICOLA: It means everything.

GIOVANNI: But how is it then that people . . . in some cases . . . give it up?

NICOLA: (*whispers*) I would myself. I'd like to be dead now! Now, this minute!

GIOVANNI: Tell me: apart from the fear, when someone knows that in a short time ... what does he think, what does he do?

NICOLA: He reckons up.

GIOVANNI: What?

NICOLA: The things he has. So that he can throw them away. Away. There's very little that really counts, you know. It's a barren field. It seemed so much, and it's nothing. Let it go, so long as ...

GIOVANNI: So long as what?

NICOLA: (*pleading*) ... So long as we're left just something! I thought ... about Vitra, where I was born. A tiny village ... with a little cat, there, in the sun; my heart bled at the thought. Then Vitra dropped from my hands too. In the end you only want ...

GIOVANNI: What?

NICOLA: To have somebody there with you. Someone who really understands you. (*Whispering*) Someone you can really trust; and tell everything to.

GIOVANNI: (*passing a hand across his face*) Yes, that's exactly what it is we want: to tell, to explain ... Nicola, when the others were in here a while ago, I wasn't being honest. But in fact ... (*He lays a hand on* NICOLA'S *shoulder.*) I ought to be grateful to you. Through you I've been given a chance ... I really craved for. Yes: I wanted something like this: to be able to go out, to meet other people, to cry out ... don't laugh.

NICOLA: (*with bent head*) No.

GIOVANNI: (*slightly pleading with him*) These years up here have been ... dreadful, did you know? My wife:

she sometimes looks at me as though she were an enemy. I had to break away. To breathe, to shout. Even if it's only an illusion, it's what I need. Do you understand me?

NICOLA: Yes.

GIOVANNI: It'll only be words, they'll laugh at me ... (*He laughs.*) But they have to be said, those words, now or never! Just to speak! Before it's too late! (*Dropping his voice a little*) My son. Outside there. One night. We were going for a walk in the dark.

NICOLA: You and your son?

GIOVANNI: Yes, after supper. Dark. Crickets singing. I was leading him by the hand.

NICOLA: When he was little?

GIOVANNI: Yes. And suddenly he said: "Papa, where are you taking me?" I could feel his hand in mine. (*He repeats, but in his own voice*) "Papa, where are you taking me?" I'm sorry, Nicola, it's very sentimental, I know. You're the first person I've ever told.

NICOLA: Yes.

GIOVANNI: But even when he was younger still, he often used to call to me ...

NICOLA: Your son?

GIOVANNI: Yes. "Papa. Papa." And I ... it's curious, I only realised afterwards ... I'd look up and feel ... a sort of anxiety. It wasn't that he wanted anything in particular. "Papa. Papa." As if he were asking, oh, I don't know, for an explanation. Or as if he wanted to tell me ... (*in a very low voice*) ... who he was, what he wanted. But I hadn't the patience, I didn't pay attention; I never knew. He is the only person I've ever loved. Really loved ... Nicola.

NICOLA: Yes?

GIOVANNI: That last night . . .

NICOLA: The night he . . .?

GIOVANNI: Yes. We were just going out, I and my wife. He looked at me.

NICOLA: Your son?

GIOVANNI: Yes. Luisa doesn't know. He looked at me for a moment, timidly. I ought to have taken notice, realised, answered. And instead . . . (*He sighs.*)

NICOLA: It was an accident?

GIOVANNI: Yes. He died. And so we couldn't ever . . . explain. (*Almost crying out*) That's what's needed, don't you see? *That!* Nothing else matters half so much. To reassure one another. To answer each other. Perhaps only *you* can listen to me and not laugh. Everyone has, inside himself . . . what shall I call it? A piece of good news! Everyone is . . . a very great, very important character! (*He laughs.*) Yes, that's what we have to tell them up there! (*As though dictating to a crowd*) Every man must be persuaded—even if he's in rags—that he's immensely, immensely important! Everyone must respect him; and make him respect himself too. They must listen to him attentively. Don't stand on top of him, don't stand in his light. But look at him with deference. Give him great, great hopes, he needs them . . . especially if he's young. Spoil him! Yes, make him grow proud! You too, Nicola, you yourself must have confidence again. And so must Luisa, poor Luisa. So must I. So must everyone.

NICOLA: (*in a low voice*) So you're actually going?

GIOVANNI: Certainly. Why shouldn't it happen, sooner or later; the Great Thaw, the Recovery?

NICOLA: (*as before*) What shall you say?

GIOVANNI: I shall say . . . (*He laughs and then, as though dictating*) Whoever gives orders shall always be slightly apologetic at having to give them. Every man's *word* is alone, he's born alone, he dies alone; give him a little space, don't deafen him by this perpetual stamping of feet. When you meet a man, don't think "What use can I make of this man?" Think it even less when he's someone who has to obey you. Perhaps we need to learn the true way to love those we love, so that they don't lose their pride . . . (*He breaks off, struck by the other's appearance.*) What's the matter, Nicola?

NICOLA: (*hoarsely*) Giovanni, after all . . . *I* ought to have been doing this.

GIOVANNI: (*observing him*) But you weren't fit enough. It's already decided.

NICOLA: Giovanni, you know, it's going to be a very tricky business.

GIOVANNI: (*still observing him*) Tricky? Why should it be? What do you mean, what's the matter?

NICOLA *is about to reply, but breaks off as he turns and sees* TOMASO *coming back.*

TOMASO: (*at the door, coming into the room; to* GIOVANNI) The press are here. You'll speak to them as we agreed; you can express yourself quite freely. We shall be present. So will Nicola.

He turns to the back. Introduced by RANIERO, *who stands aside to let them in, two men emerge from the dark fields, cross, and enter the next room.* LUISA *has appeared on the stairs;* ROSA *at the door at the back.* TOMASO *makes a polite sign to* GIOVANNI *to precede him.* GIOVANNI *follows the newspapermen. So does* NICOLA.

TOMASO: (*preparing to follow them, turns to* ROSA) What do you want? Your patient will be restored to you directly.

ROSA: (*anxiously*) But I . . . it was only that . . . as you know, I'd like to . . .

TOMASO: (*as he goes*) You can like to later on. Please be patient. (*He too withdraws into the next room.*)

ROSA: (*to* LUISA, *pointing*) What do you think they're doing in there?

LUISA: I think they're deciding.

ROSA: Deciding what?

LUISA: (*her eyes fixed on the next room*) I don't know exactly. There were a lot of things waiting to be settled. And I think they'll all be decided about and settled tonight. It will be a relief. Things couldn't have gone on like this.

ROSA: What do you mean? What are they going to settle?

LUISA: Everything.

ROSA: But before they do anything, there's something I'm sure I ought to say.

LUISA: (*turns and looks at her*) To whom?

ROSA: To your husband, I think.

LUISA: What is it?

ROSA: It's silly, perhaps. But I feel anxious about it. I don't want there to be any danger.

LUISA: Danger to whom?

ROSA: Anyone, but especially the invalid gentleman, Nicola. I had orders not to let him out of my sight. I have to look after him.

LUISA: Is he a relation of yours?

ROSA: No. I recognised him when they brought him in.

LUISA: Where?

ROSA: Into the hospital. I just happened to look up. There were three people standing round him; doctors. But he . . . was looking at me. Though he didn't know me. It was the face of a very frightened man.

LUISA: Frightened of what?

ROSA: You know what sick people are like. They plead with you; they're very crafty. Most of them beg you to tell them what's wrong with them. But that man . . . sitting there, with the three doctors round him . . . was looking at me, staring at me silently. It was very strange. (*She drops her voice.*) As if he were crying: "You: help me. You: help me." It twisted my heart.

LUISA: Why have they brought him here?

ROSA: I don't know. That night I woke up. We were alone. He was looking at me, from his bed. "You: help me. You: help me." So I . . .

LUISA: (*curiously*) Yes? You what?

ROSA: Well . . . You know when children are playing on the edge of a pool? A little brother and sister, perhaps. And the little brother falls in. And his little sister jumps in after him. And she gets drowned as well: because she can't swim. Why does she jump in? (*A brief pause.*) Just because her little brother has looked at her. "Help! Please, please! The black water's swallowing me up! I'm dying, don't leave me!" And his little sister can't bear it.

LUISA: Can't bear what?

ROSA: The baby to think he's being left. I took that

man's hand in mine. It was to tell him to keep calm. (*She laughs.*) And now he trusts me completely. When you see someone trusts you, you begin to feel frightened: it's because you feel responsible for them. There's a pact between you. (*She laughs.*) Just like a mother and son. We've never said anything about it, but I shan't leave him.

LUISA: (*almost absently, to herself*) I was really a mother, but I couldn't jump down.

ROSA: (*suddenly rapt, ardent and humble*) I would like to be very brave and heroic. I remember a place in the forest at Vinnia, full of tall silent trees. And I saw a ray of sunlight slanting down, motionless, through a space high up in them. How lovely it was! And I thought: oh, if I could be like that! But heaven is lovelier still. Every thought we have adds another mansion to it. I want to be courageous and sincere. I don't grow old and feel myself growing sly and cunning. (*Pause: she turns with a smile, to* LUISA.) It's so lovely when you feel simply from the tone of people's voices, that they respect you, isn't it? I would like the Lord to approve of me. (*She laughs.*) And my father. (*She calls*) Papa. Papa.

LUISA: Is your father dead?

ROSA: Yes.

LUISA: Do you ever pretend you're talking to him?

ROSA: Yes. Everyone who loses somebody they really care for does that in secret, didn't you know?

LUISA: Of course. I do myself . . . I do more: I invent absurd details. Like someone giving Guido a puppy; or that he's begun to shave. (*She laughs.*) When I go to sleep at night, I break off as if I were leaving something in a book to mark the place. For example, I might see you and say: "Good afternoon, have you brought me any news of my son?"

ROSA: (*after a second's pause*) Yes, he's very well.

The two women laugh.

LUISA: He's just your age. Aren't you engaged?

ROSA: We are thinking about it.

They laugh again.

LUISA: You're a good girl. (*Goes over to her and kisses her.*) Beautiful kind eyes you have. When you pretend you're talking to your father, do you feel he's near you?

ROSA: Of course. "Papa. Papa."

LUISA: "Guido. Guido."

ROSA: It's an illusion; but there's something true in it. (*Dropping her voice*) He's here. Listen.

LUISA: "Guido. Guido." It's different for me. (*Lightly*) Perhaps I'm simply rehearsing.

ROSA: Rehearsing for what?

LUISA: For when I go mad, as I shall do very soon. (*Lightly*) We are always rehearsing: even for death. We look in the glass, and arrange our expression.

ROSA: (*distressed*) But what is it you really want?

LUISA: (*lightly*) Just to understand one particular thing. Nothing happens without a reason for it. And anyway . . . (*She shrugs her shoulders and utters a long laugh.*) I'm an actress twice over. It's not true.

ROSA: What isn't?

LUISA: That I think it's possible to talk to Guido. Guido just isn't there for me. He doesn't hear. He doesn't come. It's all empty, it's all useless. Nothing. I don't believe in it. (*She controls herself.*) It's merely acting at acting. Giovanni acts too; he pretends to scold me;

but if he'd ever really told me to stop, I would have done. He too knows it's all pointless. He acts too. It's strange, isn't it? There's something . . . twisted about it, that has to be put straight. (*Pause; she hums the song.*) The fact is that Guido: isn't here. (*She calls softly*) "Guido?" Nothing.

ROSA: (*astounded and agonised*) Why not?

LUISA: Perhaps it's because: we saw him, afterwards. He was . . . so shattered. When anyone falls from a height like that . . . they look as if they'd been crushed. Giovanni says: "run over." It wasn't Guido's face any more. Seeing anything like that . . . (*in a very low voice*) it's difficult to have any hope at all. It would be terrible to see him rise from the dead. I don't know whether he . . . knew . . . that he'd have to rise again one day. Perhaps he'd never been told that. That's why I think that suddenly at the last moment, he was terrified . . . and shouted. (*Imitates*) Aaaah! He was terribly shattered.

ROSA: (*whispering and smiling almost roguishly*) But what about the soul? That is never shattered. It's like a marvellous coloured fire . . . No: every soul is like a tiny drop without which the whole universe would thirst. Souls are flowers. That's why we must never hurt them in any way.

LUISA: Do you long for your father?

ROSA: Yes. I say to him: "Papa, stay with me a little." He goes away, but I feel comforted just the same.

LUISA: How did he die?

ROSA: I can remember it well. Like someone reaching the top of a beautiful hill.

LUISA: There was nothing like that in our case. If

Guido had a soul, his soul doesn't haunt the dreams in this house. We spend our lives inviting him here, but without belief. (*Suddenly dropping her voice, and trembling*) I think ... that he is reproaching us for something; that's what it is really. We did something to him, we hurt him in some way, that's the trouble. Oh, my God, there's no cure for it, there's no cure.

ROSA: (*smiles as before, and recites in gentle tones*) "I thank Thee that Thou hast created me and kept this night for me; may Thy mercy be ever with me and with them I love" ... (*She makes a little sign for* LUISA *to listen, and draws from her pocket a little book, from which she reads*) "I believe in the resurrection. I believe Thou wilt give, to each according to his deserts, punishment and reward. In accordance with this faith I desire to live, to deserve true life ... so that I may not wander confused through eternity." ... (*Raises her head.*) Yes: I don't want to be timid and afraid any more. I will do my duty.

LUISA: (*with rebellious hostility*) And what is it? What is this important thing you have to tell my husband? I'll tell him myself.

ROSA: I ought to tell him that Nicola ... it's quite true he's very shaken now, he's become so, but ...

LUISA: Well?

ROSA: He's not ill. He's not ill. He pretends to be. The others pretend to believe him. But he's not ill. I'm sure there's something terribly dangerous going on here ...

LUISA: Dangerous for whom?

ROSA: ... and I'm sure there may be serious consequences ...

Voices and footsteps are heard approaching from the next room.

LUISA: I will tell my husband myself.

ROSA: (*retreating to the back*) For heaven's sake, please tell him. Please. Warn him.

LUISA: Don't worry.

ROSA *vanishes into the night. At the same moment, all the men who have been in the next room re-enter: the two journalists,* GIOVANNI, TOMASO, NICOLA, *and* RANIERO. *The group crosses in silence, like some solemn procession, to the outer doors. Here in a strangely ceremonious way, a series of goodbyes is made, their centre being* GIOVANNI. *Finally the two journalists depart into the dark.*

GIOVANNI: (*lightly*) Well, there was something almost macabre about the whole thing, didn't you think? My statement sounded like the last wishes of the dying. And those goodbyes . . . they seemed like—— (*He meets his wife's gaze.*) Is there something the matter, Luisa?

LUISA: (*after a moment*) No, nothing.

GIOVANNI: Do you know what we're going to do?

LUISA: I heard. (*She goes and sits down at some distance from them.*)

GIOVANNI *looks at her, and then looks at* TOMASO, *who is at the outer doors, talking in a low voice to two of his men, who have appeared from outside.*

TOMASO: (*turns to* GIOVANNI) I'm just giving a few final instructions. (*Comes into the centre.*) Well, the newspapermen have gone. The hardest part's over; the letter's in the post. The tinder's alight. And now, everyone else not primarily concerned will also leave us. And so, little by little, everything goes according to plan.

The night will soon be over; we have only a few hours morc to wait.

GIOVANNI: (*lightly*) You've rather a funereal air about you, too. But then, you usually have.

TOMASO: Yes. It's my way of avoiding the lofty manner. (*Suddenly turning to* NICOLA) Right then, Nicola. You go on down. The car's waiting for you. Look after yourself. Get well again.

NICOLA: Yes, I shall have to rest. Goodbye for the present, Giovanni. I hope you understand. The state I'm in . . .

TOMASO: We've already eviscerated that point. Goodbye.

ROSA: (*appearing in the doorway*) I'm here, Mr. Nicola. Come along. I'll take your arm.

TOMASO: No. (*To* NICOLA) We've arranged for you to go back by yourself, Nicola. (*A silence.*)

NICOLA: (*hoarsely*) Oh, why?

TOMASO: Organisational necessities. You'll travel with the doctor. It's only half an hour's journey. You'll have your little angel back with you, the minute you get down there.

NICOLA: (*in a strange voice*) But . . . what . . . why is this?

TOMASA: It'll be best for the doctor to be with you. You're over-excited.

NICOLA: (*stammering slightly*) But I don't want . . . I can't . . . I'm only well when Rosa's there . . . I want to go down with her. Rosa! Rosa!

ROSA: (*coming forward*) Mr. Nicola is quite right. It helps him when I'm there. I won't leave him, whatever you say. I want to stay with him.

TOMASO: (*with genuine sadness*) Faithful, kind protectress, you must do as I say. It has already been decided. It is part of the arrangements. We must take all precautions against even an indirect leakage. Secrecy is everything in these cases. We also have to consider the possibility of hostile action; it's only a matter of a few minutes. (*Pause.*) Nicola will tell you the same.

NICOLA: (*suddenly, in a different voice*) Yes, Rosa, we shall be together again very soon; we'll be able to talk; you shall read to me. Thank you, Rosa most lovable, Rosa, my shining one. Go on, you'd better hurry. Wrap up warm. (*Pause while* ROSA *goes out, escorted by one of* TOMASO's *men.*) And now I must go, too. Good night, gentlemen. Don't think too badly of me. Every effort to keep alive implies a certain loss of style—and not always with success. Unfortunately, the whole of geography, the whole of history ... (*pointing upwards*) and astronomy, are contained in the kernel of our lives. If I lose that I lose everything. But let's hope for the best, I don't feel ill now. (*He turns on his way to the door.*) I shall give up politics for good; I shall go back to Vitra, it's only a tiny place. Goodbye.

He goes out, not without dignity, followed by RANIERO *and the other man.*

TOMASO: (*to* GIOVANNI) He is in such a state of excitement we had to take special precautions. (*He begins to murmur the melody of Guido's song between his teeth.*)

GIOVANNI: (*who has gone to look out at the back*) What's happening down there? They're all leaving, without headlights.

RANIERO *re-enters and sits down.*

TOMASO: The principal characters remain: we three. (*He notices* LUISA.) Oh, and your wife. But she belongs here. (*He resumes his humming.*)

LUISA *rises in silence and goes into the next room.*

GIOVANNI: (*with a final glance out*) So here we are then, alone. (*He looks at his watch.*) And two hours to wait.

TOMASO: The minute the first ray of light falls on the front of the house, we shall hear a signal. We shall go outside. You will stand in the doorway and wave a white cloth. The others over there will do the same: a signal of peace. The fields will be deserted, just three little dots in the middle of them: ourselves. But there'll be plenty of binoculars trained on us from the distance. History is waiting.

GIOVANNI: It's all been very well organised.

TOMASO: Like clockwork.

GIOVANNI: I could use these two hours to go down to the village.

TOMASO: I must ask you not to, I'm afraid. You'd only lay yourself open to questions. In any case, what for?

GIOVANNI: I'd like to make a telephone call.

TOMASO: I'm afraid they've cut off the telephone as well. We had to.

GIOVANNI: Oh, quite. It was simply for the sake of the walk.

RANIERO: If you want to go for a walk I'll come with you. You'll find me outside here. (*He goes out.*)

TOMASO: (*moving after him*) I'm sorry, Giovanni; but what we're starting up here after all has a certain importance. We've had to take the greatest precautions.

GIOVANNI: Quite.

TOMASO: The signal-box has also been evacuated. (*With the faintest shade of deliberateness*) Our friends are watching, they're scattered about everywhere. (*He goes out.*)

GIOVANNI: (*alone, sits down, lost in thought; suddenly turns and listens; rises slowly and whispers*) Who's that?

ROSA: (*furtively, and rather dishevelled, appears at one of the outer doors; she is out of breath, and pauses a moment before answering*) I waited till you were alone. (*A pause.*) Nicola is dead. As soon as he went out. I'm afraid he's been killed. (*Coming nearer*) I managed to catch his last words. I ran away to tell you. They were meant for you.

GIOVANNI: What did he want you to tell me?

ROSA: He said he begged you to forgive him. He said the hope of living confused him. He said that you, and not he, will be . . .

GIOVANNI: (*stops her with his hand; slowly*) . . . the incident.

ROSA: Another Andrea the Baker; he said you will also tip the scales, in the same way, only with much more noise.

GIOVANNI: (*thinks for a moment*) Thank you. It's a good thing you hurried back; I only hope you won't pay too heavily for it. (*He opens one of the side-doors.*) Go and hide in there.

ROSA *goes through the door.*

GIOVANNI: (*calls through the same door*) Luisa! (*He goes across to look out at the back for a moment, then begins hastily rummaging in a side-board.*)

LUISA: (*coming in*) What is it?

GIOVANNI: (*in low tones*) Luisa, I've got to get out of this. I'm just taking a bit of food, and a lantern, help me; I shall go down along the Foss-way. I know the whole place—no one will get me. (*Pointing*) They're strolling outside there, I shall take the opportuunity to slip away now.

LUISA: And tomorrow: what about the meeting?

GIOVANNI: (*still rummaging*) They were fixing up an incident to prevent it. A dead man. They were going to blame those over there for it. The spark for the great explosion, that's what they were after. "Only out of cataclysm is anything new born." That's their idea.

LUISA: (*mechanically helping him*) What about you?

GIOVANNI: (*as he packs*) Me? I was to be the dead man. I refuse. And before I refused, Nicola refused, without much success. If I go away, the whole thing will break down. In any case this farce doesn't depend on me. (*A little excited*) Very funny, the whole thing! This is really what they mean when they talk about turning the priest's cowl inside out, putting arsenic in the Host and dragging the universe along by the nose! And I was to be the Host and the arsenic, the cheese in the trap, the worm on the pin.

LUISA: Where will you go?

GIOVANNI: It'll be difficult to keep alive. But it'll be better than sacrificing oneself to *this*!

LUISA: And what will happen here?

GIOVANNI: (*inattentively*) You've got enough money . . . (*Then, noticing what she has said*) What do you mean? You'll shut the place up and go away.

LUISA: I didn't mean me . . . I meant . . . our own

problem . . . our son. What's happened has happened, hasn't it? That's all. (*A pause.*)

GIOVANNI: Luisa. (*For the first time a painful vehemence carries him away.*) Luisa, we've stood there for years, looking down there, over that dreadful flower-bed!

LUISA: (*remains calm*) Yes, because there was something . . . that wasn't clear. And now if you go away, I shall be left alone thinking about it. But it's too big a problem for me. I might even forget about it, too, and then . . .

GIOVANNI: Luisa! Luisa! (*Controlling himself*) There has never been any problem. There's only been . . . (*Suddenly overcome*) Yes, torture! Torture every day, every hour, year after year . . . Luisa, you've broken me, destroyed me, you've managed to——

LUISA: I don't believe it, you're too strong. No one can break you. (*She thinks for a moment.*) But you can break others.

GIOVANNI: What do you mean?

LUISA: I can't even think any more. I can only do what you tell me to. It was the same with Guido. And what shall I do now? I'm frightened . . . they'll shut me up . . . and I shall grow old, screaming, with my hair matted together, getting greyer . . .

GIOVANNI: Luisa, I beg you, I implore you, to keep calm.

LUISA: Oh, but I am. It's only . . . that problem.

GIOVANNI: (*trying to control her by an intense effort at persuasion*) Luisa: I can't just let myself be killed. And I can't allow this crime they're plotting. It isn't any choice of mine. It's them, they've forced me to it. They came up here . . .

LUISA: (*quietly, with great simplicity*) Yes. To punish you.

GIOVANNI: (*arrested*) Punish me? Why?

LUISA: Nothing. I just said it. (*But she smiles and repeats*) Yes, they came to punish you.

GIOVANNI: What on earth do you mean? Punish me for what?

LUISA: For what you did.

GIOVANNI: What did I do? Luisa, you've never spoken to me like this before.

LUISA: I know, because in all these years we have never said what ought to have been said. We've never been honest.

GIOVANNI: And what ought to have been said?

LUISA: That someone must have been responsible, there couldn't not have been someone. It would have been absurd.

GIOVANNI: And who was it?

LUISA: You.

GIOVANNI: Responsible for what?

LUISA: Guido. And for everything else.

GIOVANNI: Oh. In what way?

LUISA: I believe ... yes, I believe you hated him. Yes. Perhaps you always hated him. It was you, wasn't it? It was you who shut him in that night.

GIOVANNI: Luisa, you must be raving mad.

LUISA: But why did you lock him in?

GIOVANNI: I never thought.

LUISA: But why should you lock him in and never think? Because you hated him. You bullied him. I know how you used to look at him.

GIOVANNI: Whatever do you mean, Luisa? Do you want to send me mad as well? Why did I hate him?

LUISA: Because you . . . you hated me as well, didn't you? You used to speak to me gently, and never look at me. You want everything your own way. You hate everything that's near to you. He died because of you.

GIOVANNI: You're talking madness, you know you are.

LUISA: (*raising her voice for the first time*) Yes, you killed him! You were responsible. It was your doing. And now you want to run away.

GIOVANNI: Luisa, talk quietly.

LUISA: Murderer! Oh, why did I ever meet you! Why did I ever have a child! Why was I born! Oh, my God, what's going to become of me? Oh, how horrible it is, how horrible! (*She drops, sobbing, on to the table, her head buried in her arms.*)

GIOVANNI *looks at her; his gaze turns to the outer doors, where at any moment* TOMASO *may appear; he hesitates a moment; then flees.*

LUISA: (*sobs to herself; then she rises and wipes her eyes; goes to the door and calls*) Tomaso! (*She comes back to the middle of the room.*)

TOMASO: (*as he comes in*) What's the matter?

LUISA: (*calmly pointing*) My husband: he's found out. He's run away. If you want to catch him, he told me he would go along the Foss-way. You'll easily catch him, he's only just gone. (*A silence.*)

TOMASO *moves back to the outer doors, to summon* RANIERO, *but suddenly stops.* GIOVANNI *has reappeared out of the darkness, and is slowly returning to the doorway.*

CURTAIN

ACT THREE

Only a few moments have passed. GIOVANNI *and* TOMASO *are facing each other;* LUISA *stands some distance away from them.*

GIOVANNI: (*coming forward; to* TOMASO, *quietly*) So one of you would have had to kill me.

TOMASO: (*simply, almost sadly*) Yes.

GIOVANNI: Who?

TOMASO: Oh, someone; whoever was ordered to.

GIOVANNI: How? Where?

TOMASO: (*is silent for a moment; then pointing*) There; tomorrow morning, the minute you appeared in the doorway.

GIOVANNI: What had I done to deserve it?

TOMASO: Given big orders; known important secrets: it's almost right, surely, that it should cost something in the end?

GIOVANNI: And you were going to accuse . . .

TOMASO: Our enemies.

GIOVANNI: And after that: war.

TOMASO: It was thought that that would probably happen.

GIOVANNI: And so you were deceiving me: completely.

TOMASO: Keeping you in the dark made the thing a little easier for all of us. Yours isn't the only difficult job in this. Now the whole thing will be harder.

GIOVANNI: And the thought of the consequences didn't deter you?

TOMASO: (*still in his usual slightly melancholy tones*) It seems that history doesn't develop simply by accidents; something more unpleasant seems to be needed. Besides every mine has to have a fuse attached to it: an expedient; often a sad one. But perhaps action is always sad. And stupid.

RANIERO *has appeared in the doorway.*

GIOVANNI: (*to* RANIERO) And the decision rested with just you two?

TOMASO: (*replying for* RANIERO) There was no question of decisions at this point. It was only a question of carrying them out. (*To* RANIERO, *but without looking at him*) Come in, Raniero. We were only here to obey, that's all.

RANIERO: (*looking down*) The less we talk, the better.

GIOVANNI: And all those people asleep in their beds, down there? They were to suffer the consequences of all this tomorrow, were they not? They might have been consulted, I can't help thinking.

TOMASO: They were. It was precisely they who decided all this, long ago. For years past, their footsteps and ours, consciously or otherwise, have been moving in this direction. (*Lowering his voice*) Why did you try to run away? (GIOVANNI *looks at him without answering.*) For one thing, I credited you with more self-control. I told you there were guards, everywhere.

GIOVANNI: Nevertheless, I came back of my own accord.

TOMASO: For what reason?

GIOVANNI: I suddenly felt weary at the very thought

of flight. It is always exhausting; foolish as well. ... Don't go, Luisa, I'd rather you stayed.

LUISA *has moved towards the stairs. At his words she turns back.*

GIOVANNI: (*continuing; to* TOMASO) So that the moment I'd got over the first physical panic, I no longer wanted to turn my back on things. You were quite right, Luisa: everything has to be settled and finished with; we couldn't go on like that. And you are right, Tomaso. I'm in on this, too. (*Pause.*) I have to say my say also. (*A silence.*)

TOMASO: (*almost amiably*) Giovanni. It may well be that this unexpected turn does make a certain re-examination of the situation necessary. (*In low tones*) But in any case you will not yourself be free to make any personal choice. You would only be lowering yourself if you tried to. (*He breaks off.*)

ROSA *has slowly opened the door and stands there.*

TOMASO: ... Ah, Rosa. You're here too. (*With restrained coldness*) Why did you come back? You had had your orders.

ROSA: (*attempting to speak*) Nicola ...

TOMASO: (*interrupting her with a gesture*) Yes, Nicola. Nicola is dead. (*To* GIOVANNI) First of all he was indiscreet; and then when he found we knew, he tried cunning; but he was not cunning enough. He opposed me, and then agreed with me, and betrayed you ... a deplorable man, and always a menace. A dangerous character. And above all, cowardly.

ROSA: But I ...

TOMASO: (*silencing her once more*) You should have confined yourself to being faithful. Nothing further was required of you.

ROSA: (*with a stifled cry*) Faithful to whom?

TOMASO: (*looks at her for a moment.*) To your father, for one thing. Do you know how your father really died? Do you know that Nicola was one of the people responsible?

ROSA: I know. (*Pause.*) Nicola told me, as he died.

TOMASO: (*indicating* GIOVANNI) And that he was another of them?

ROSA: Yes. And that you were another.

TOMASO: (*with sudden amiability*) Well, in that case you'll have realised . . . that it isn't any business of yours to try and understand the real significance of these things. I must ask you not to interfere. Giovanni, you will have no allies.

RANIERO: Tomaso.

TOMASO: Yes?

RANIERO: What's going on?

TOMASO: Nothing.

RANIERO: But all this talk; and before as well. What are we to do about Giovanni? I'd feel better if things were a bit more straightforward.

TOMASO: Naturally.

RANIERO: And what are these two women going to say tomorrow, and later on?

TOMASO: Tomorrow, and later on, there will probably be such a row going on, that it will take something louder than the voices of a couple of women to make anyone listen. Nothing's going on, Raniero. We always had to allow for a certain amount of . . . inconvenience. All it calls for is . . .

GIOVANNI: (*enigmatically*) A little more determination on your part.

TOMASO: (*after a pause*) Yes. Exactly. Well then, Raniero, I'd like to know what you think. About what's to be done.

RANIERO: (*head bent*) But I . . .

TOMASO: Do we have to give up our . . . expedient . . . and go back? That would mean not only disobeying our orders; it would mean confessing to the world an overture which the world would certainly regard as contemptible; and, moreover, confessing that it had failed. It would mean irreparable damage to our own people and an immense gift to the others. And finally it would put us, and I mean us personally, in a very precarious position: the witnesses to certain kinds of exploit rarely survive.

GIOVANNI: (*enigmatically*) As we learn from Nicola.

TOMASO: (*still to* RANIERO) The alternative is: to go up there, and negotiate the agreement. Which means? It means filling in a few days with hypocritical toasts and lies, and then finding ourselves where we were before, with an even lower view of mankind than when we started. *Bos. Pecus:* Yes, gentlemen. Besides, in view of what our orders are, that would be even more seditious. It would also give our enemies an opportunity of playing, in their own good time, exactly the game we'd abandoned.

GIOVANNI: (*enigmatically*) That has often happened.

TOMASO: (*still to* RANIERO) Well, Raniero? What do you think?

RANIERO: (*head bent*) That we'd better finish what we've started.

TOMASO: Good, Raniero: excellent. That's my own opinion. (*Mildly satirical*) So: the Executive has deliberated. As I always say: everything is going according to plan, of itself. (*Pause.*) And so . . . the thing will go on. It will proceed exactly as arranged. (*Dropping his voice slightly*) It would not be decent to retreat; on anyone's part.

RANIERO: (*worried*) But why all this talk?

TOMASO: Because the earth goes round so slowly. I imagine that at this moment, a thousand miles further east, the mountains are already shining in the sun. In half an hour's time it will be the same here. The light will give us the strength we need.

RANIERO: Half an hour to wait. Thirty long minutes.

TOMASO: (*looking at him*) I know what you mean, Raniero. It certainly isn't the best sort of time for us to start . . . putting fleas in one another's ears.

RANIERO: (*with a sudden shiver of fear*) It isn't my fault.

TOMASO: Yes, Raniero. You are all for direct action. (*Pause.*) I give you permission to hesitate. (*Pause.*) Hesitate, by all means. (*Pause.*) I will even excuse you from acting at all. Everything will be exactly the same without you. Giovanni hasn't expressed any opinion; but he can have no influence on what will happen; within half an hour things will begin to move. (*He at last turns to* GIOVANNI; *a pause.*) Yes, Giovanni, you will have to submit. You will have no supporters. I know your objections: they're a wind that's been blowing for centuries; and they've never dislodged so much as a single stone. People repeat them and never believe in them. And you yourself . . . (*Intensely persuasive*) Look: it's not that I've any wish to convince you; but you yourself really want to agree with me. You can't go against us—and how could you? I should be interested to know—you can't go against us: because you don't wish to. You find it restful, just obeying orders. (*Dropping his voice*) Because deep down, you don't believe in the game either.

GIOVANNI: (*suddenly, half-nonchalantly*) Do you?

TOMASO: (*suddenly turns and looks at* GIOVANNI; *then paces a moment about the room.*) I? . . . I. (*He laughs lightly; then speaks as before.*) I was simply saying, as before, that there's no more to discuss. Orders, promises, duty, decency, everything demands that we should——

GIOVANNI: But *do* you believe it?

TOMASO: (*looks at* GIOVANNI *again, and ponders for a moment.*) Clever Giovanni. A curious question: in the very last half-hour. A curious conversation. But perhaps you are right. This is the moment for it. (*With mild irony*) Now or never. (*To the others*) One moment, ladies and gentlemen. I'd like you all to be seated. (*Almost shouting*) Yes, why don't you sit down? (*Calmly once more*) Sit. Please, sit down.

Some of them do so; but not GIOVANNI.

RANIERO: (*perturbed*) What is all this?

TOMASO: This. In the first place I ought to inform you that we are all excused from having to act. Not only Raniero, but all of us. We are spectators: we shall do no more than watch, or very little more. And naturally, we shall also submit. (*Pause.*) How can you ever have imagined that so important a result could have been left to depend on some chance oscillation, yours, or his, or even mine; or on something unforeseen? And with so slender a margin of safety? For goodness' sake. No, gentlemen. We had to be completely, super-abundantly *certain* about this from the start. Don't worry, Giovanni: you will probably not be alone: it's possible that quite a number of us here may also be dead in a very short time; we shall have drunk our hemlock. Knowing the way things go, I think it more than likely. And the door is blocked up behind our backs. The matter is no longer in our hands. It's its own master; it goes by itself; nothing can stop it now.

RANIERO: And what about us?

TOMASO: We don't count any longer. And so—this is the point—we are offered a unique opportunity: a quarter of an hour to be really quiet in. A point of real silence; all our worries are over: a great calm. It would be unforgivable not to take advantage of it.

RANIERO: To do what?

TOMASO: To try to understand. Why don't you sit down too, Giovanni? Let's make the most of these few minutes. You too will have to drink your hemlock; you cannot prevent it.

LUISA *raises her head; after a moment, as in the first act, she goes to the sideboard, and takes out glasses and a bottle; in a profound silence, she puts them on the table, methodically placing small table-napkins beside them.*

TOMASO: Giovanni, you asked me if I believed in all this . . . (*He reflects for a moment.*) Well, I'll tell you . . . What's happening to me is this: at the point we've now come to, I'm tempted to enjoy myself a little: yes. This calm night . . . this gentle breeze . . . interest me almost more than the other thing. I find them relaxing; I'm enjoying them. As for the other thing . . . perhaps none of us believes in it. Perhaps even Raniero doesn't.

GIOVANNI: All the same you've taken a great deal of trouble over it. A lifetime, just to get to this. Your life's work.

TOMASO: A whole lifetime. (*Blandly ironic*) My dear Giovanni, the dark is already beginning to lift slightly, and I think that in a short time, I can begin to reveal a secret to you: (*pause*) that though I may perhaps have given myself a great deal of trouble . . . I've never done anything! You too have been a leader; and an intelligent one; and you're now a retired one; and even at the very end, you still haven't realised? Action is a dream. We see hands move: and they're not ours. The gestures of a dream.

GIOVANNI: All the same, there are gestures and days that can fill us with terror for the rest of our lives.

TOMASO: The terror of dreams. Ideas: we find them here, inside our foreheads, like a pasteboard jewel left on the table by someone else. Astonished witnesses, we look at events, and the fact of looking at them makes them exist, and it's as though we were remembering them. The events of a dream.

GIOVANNI: All the same, we add something of our own to them.

TOMASO: Nothing, Giovanni. Let's admit it once and for all. What we did . . . no, we cannot swear that it was right, or even useful.

RANIERO: (*in distress*) What then?

TOMASO: (*with a shrug*) It didn't depend on us. Only on itself. It was going where it had to. (*Blandly ironic*) And the thing that's going to happen here now . . .

no, there's no certainty that it may not be very ugly indeed.

RANIERO: Why do you only say this now?

TOMASO: Because it can't do any harm to say it now. One couldn't before. The dawn is already beginning to lighten; and that allows us at last to be sincere. (*With a touch of amazement*) Perhaps I never have been that. Sincere; and free. I owe it to something waiting up there on the hills. A weapon. We are excused; that will look after everything; a weapon, pointed just there at the door.

ROSA: Where from?

TOMASO: From so far away that the shooting will not even be a crime; it will be only a matter of skill; we shall hardly hear the shot. Or shots, as the case may be. Yes, it's not certain that only one of us will fall. In cases as important as this any attempt at economy is inadvisable. A fine mechanism! Technically, I'm very proud of it. And apart from that, do you know what? I've suspected it all my life, tonight I'm certain: apart from that, nothing much matters to me.

ROSA: (*timidly to* GIOVANNI; *touching him*) And you! Are you going to let this happen? You'll be more responsible for it than anyone if it does!

TOMASO: Responsibility. (*Suddenly*) But where is it, what is it? What a curious misunderstanding ... (*To* LUISA) Madam: do you really think there is some point in scrabbling in that flower-bed of yours? Or anywhere else?

ROSA: (*timidly to* GIOVANNI, *in a whisper*) I ran back on purpose. And Nicola wanted to warn you as he lay dying. And you came back on purpose: so that this shouldn't happen. It's wrong, it's wrong.

TOMASO: Wrong! Grass, grubs in the earth; all come

to nothing; and know nothing of right and wrong. And in what way do we differ from them? Life: of itself: devours the field as it passes over it.

GIOVANNI: (*lost in thought*) Lays it waste.

TOMASO: And everything obeys. And children fall and die. But that's the fate of everything else too. There is nothing else. And why should man be the only exception? No. We roll docilely down the same slope. There was a push, at the beginning. And we—human beings, plants, planets . . .

GIOVANNI: Are simply wearing it away. (*He looks towards the mountains.*) The mountains erode and change their outline . . . (*Vaguely raising his glass*) But you up there, mountains!—you never notice . . . that's the point, Tomaso. They are not aware of the fact. And we are. Which means . . . (*He breaks off; thoughtfully*) Luisa. You said I hated him. Why?

LUISA: I don't know.

GIOVANNI: You said I hated everything. Why?

LUISA: (*a cry*) I don't know!

The first light has appeared on the mountains.

GIOVANNI: (*looking towards them*) In a splendid blaze of light, the universe goes on its way unknowing: unknowing it was begun only that it might be ended; that it appeared only that it might be blotted out. There is only one tiny character that knows that. We, mankind. (*Pause.*) That's where the great torment stings; and squeezes out a highly active brew: the drop of acid.

TOMASO: All that will be settled tomorrow. You cannot obstruct it.

GIOVANNI: . . . Hate, yes, hate. The drop of pollution.

There's a taste of it in every glass. We put it there. The rest . . . (*he looks towards the mountain-tops*) is flavourless. Only for us, blood . . . goes flowing on till it makes the flower-beds fester. Luisa, why did you say it was I that killed him?

LUISA: I don't remember.

GIOVANNI: What action or influence did you attribute to me?

LUISA: Nothing, I didn't mean anything!

GIOVANNI: What made you use that word?

LUISA: (*with a cry*) Let me alone! It was I who told them——

GIOVANNI: That I was running away. Yes, I know. (*Once more addressing himself thoughtfully*) The drop of bitterness. It's the taste of the dregs. Guilt at having been there. The desire to be punished and to punish. And you, Luisa: did *you* say anything to him.

LUISA: To whom?

GIOVANNI: Guido also looked at you that night.

LUISA: Why? What should I have said to him?

GIOVANNI: (*turning away from her*) The drop of infection. A kind of virus. They pretend to be angels, but they're not, oh, no, you see it when they fall. Fevered and heavy. Not heedless; but ready and quick. Treacherous. They run, fascinated, towards any scene of disaster. They pass the contagion to each other, all of them: one will command, another obey; one will flatter, another boast: "You shall die! You shall die! You shall die!" (*To himself*) We're sick; the world is diseased. It's one vast, blighted flower-bed. It is true I hated; not Guido. But everything else I did.

TOMASO: The night is ending. It will be clear.

GIOVANNI: The responsible. The responsible. I said no to everyone. But they all said the same to me everywhere: No! No! No! No! No! (*Suddenly quiet*) Luisa.

LUISA: Yes.

A silence.

GIOVANNI: It isn't true that I locked the door when I went out.

LUISA: You . . . didn't lock it!

GIOVANNI: No. Nor the window either.

LUISA: Surely you did!

GIOVANNI: No.

LUISA: But you've always said . . .

GIOVANNI: I began by saying so, there and then. And I've gone on saying so.

LUISA: But why?

GIOVANNI: The open book: I put it there myself, in the first minutes during the confusion.

LUISA: Then . . .

GIOVANNI: I wiped out certain traces, and faked others.

LUISA: What do you mean?

GIOVANNI: The cigarettes. The boy had cigarettes; he didn't need to go out for them, he never even tried to. There were no marks on the ledge outside the window. I took the cigarettes from his pocket myself. They were soaked in blood. I made it all up.

LUISA: Why?

GIOVANNI: Because . . . I was ashamed; it's very strange. I was covered with shame. (*Half-shouting*) I wanted . . . to hide it, hide it, so that no one should ever know!

LUISA. Know what?

GIOVANNI: (*almost calmly, as though reading*) Our son wandered about his home. He sang softly to himself; looked at himself in the glass. Incredulous of himself; and of everything, an empty look . . . the look of one whose only fate is to die. Purposeless: unenduring, unredeemable: an error; and capable of knowing itself that. Destitute of title to any kind of pride or hope. A dreary weight. And so . . .

LUISA: Giovanni . . .

GIOVANNI: (*almost as though attaching no importance to it*) I wanted to tell you it wasn't I who killed him. Something worse than that happened. It was himself. He threw himself from the window.

LUISA *remains motionless and rigid.*

GIOVANNI: And everything followed quite calmly. He was fifteen. (*Overcome for an instant*) Ah! But what are you doing there, running about and shouting, don't you see what's happening? Children are refusing to live. There's nothing more to do about it, everything's wrong and rotten within! The marrow in the bone is revolting against itself, the stones are turning into toads! (*He pauses; and looks at* ROSA, *who has moved timidly forward and placed a hand on* LUISA'S *shoulder. Then he speaks almost calmly.*) Yes, Rosa. Our son looked down at the dark courtyard below. And a sort of ecstasy transformed him; and gave him the same expression the world now rushing up here has on its face. And he chose to throw himself down there. And so be it, and let there be an end. Obstruct you, Tomaso? Why should I? It's I who want it. This error has to be punished. Wiped out.

RANIERO: (*pointing outside and listening*) What's that?

TOMASO: The sun is about to rise. The leaves can feel it.

RANIERO: (*pointing*) There it is.

TOMASO: It will be here on the house in a few moments. We shall hear the signal. (*To* GIOVANNI) You will appear out there, in the doorway, waving that. (*He points to a white napkin on the table.*) And then everything will be square.

RANIERO: (*troubled*) Is it at times like this one ought to pray?

They all turn at the sound of sobbing. LUISA *is quietly weeping to herself; suddenly overcome, she cries out.*

LUISA: It was my fault! It was my fault! It was I who should have told him . . .

ROSA *gently caresses her.*

GIOVANNI: (*also overcome*) It was all of us. I, you, he, everyone. (*To* TOMASO) "Us and them"! All responsible. We all shoved him down there! All the problems are one problem, they shall all be solved together! A vast infection. Let's burn the bag of straw and the leper inside it.

LUISA: (*sobbing*) It was I! I was his mother! It was I who should have told him . . . I never did, and he's dead.

ROSA: (*stroking her*) No, no, Luisa: you will tell him everything. Not that he doesn't know by now, but perhaps . . . he'll be glad if you . . . (*She breaks off.*)

A long musical bugle-call is heard from the distance.

RANIERO: The signal.

LUISA *sobs.*

ROSA: You'll tell him . . .

GIOVANNI: (*a cry*) What! Tell him what!

ROSA: That it's a mistake to think we're not watched over, not protected. (*Pointing towards the mountains, now magnificently lit by the sun*) Do you see? Oh, wonderful! (*With a break in her voice*) Why do I tremble like this, and want to die?

The signal is heard again.

ROSA: Oh, what grace was given us when we were called on to exist and to see. (*Pause.*) Mr. Giovanni, I'm sure, I'm *sure* you won't allow this crime. You thought yourself it was right and sensible to go up there to the pass, to meet our enemies, and seek agreement with them. Why don't you do it?

GIOVANNI: It doesn't depend on me, my dear. It's something much bigger.

ROSA: But you wanted to go. Why don't you obey your own self?

GIOVANNI: Because it was foolish. I've given in.

ROSA: Are you willing for so many men to suffer and die because of you then?

GIOVANNI: But they are dead already.

ROSA: It's not true.

GIOVANNI: There is not a living soul among them.

ROSA: You know you don't think that!

The signal again, louder. At the same time the scraping sound of the wind in the branches is heard.

GIOVANNI: What will march out of this house in a few moments from now will be a procession of the dead. And I shall be fittingly at the head of them!

ROSA: It's not true. That isn't what you want. (*In different tones*) That's not what your son wanted ...

GIOVANNI: Nevertheless, he threw himself from the window. He didn't believe, not even he.

ROSA: But wouldn't you hold him back, now?

GIOVANNI: The world knows what it wants; and the world wants this.

ROSA: Then you must stop it!

The signal and the wind again, both louder.

GIOVANNI: Why should I try to? I am the worst and the least believing of the lot.

ROSA: Just to tell ...

GIOVANNI: ... tell whom?

ROSA: Your son!

GIOVANNI: But my son's not here!

ROSA: (*a cry*) But *you* are here, it's your duty! Go up there, go up and tell them to have faith. Take your place there, save them! (*A silence.*)

GIOVANNI: (*quietly*) My dear girl, how? By means of what miracle? We can do no more.

TOMASO: (*troubled*) The door was shut. And in men's souls as well.

GIOVANNI: This is the beginning of the great collapse. And what are the surroundings doing? Looking on. Grass, sky, rocks: impassively. Sumptuous indifference; rigid concatenation; everything obeying. And where is the link in the chain that shall break? Where are you, pride, hope, immortal soul? You too are here, Rosa, and what are you doing?

A silence. Then, very distantly, the signal once more.

ROSA: (*has bent her head, mortified; now she raises it.*) I ...

(*She takes a step forward.*) I . . . I do not believe that they will really shoot. I don't believe that people want to kill. They do it because they are truly, truly in a dream.

The signal again.

ROSA: (*taking another step forward*) We are in a dream; so are the others; so was your son; so is the man standing up there with the rifle. All that is needed is to wake them, to warn them. That is simple; yes, simple. I will do it, and you shall pass. They will not shoot.

She runs to the table. GIOVANNI *darts forward to stop her, but too late.*

ROSA: (*seizes the white cloth, runs to the doorway, waves it; she stays there, waiting.*) Help us, Oh Lord! Give us Your aid!

A distant shot. ROSA *staggers and falls.*

LUISA: (*catches her in her arms*) Rosa. Rosa.

TOMASO: (*in distress*) Perhaps something has gone wrong.

LUISA *raises her eyes and looks at* GIOVANNI. *The others do the same.*

GIOVANNI: Perhaps something has gone wrong. (*He moves forward; lifts the girl up, and holds her in his arms.*) Let us go, and take her with us. (*Repeating, with profound certainty*) They will not shoot. I say that now they will respect us.

TOMASO: (*little more than a nod*) Yes.

RANIERO: Yes.

LUISA *nods in agreement.* GIOVANNI, *preceding the little group and holding* ROSA *in his arms, goes out on to the threshold and waits in silence.*

The silence persists: then the signal-calls are heard again. They have, now, a festive sound.

GIOVANNI: We will go up there and say what has to be said, and they will listen to us.

They all depart towards the pass and the sound of the signals.

THE END

SUMMERTIME

(*Il Paese delle Vacanze*)

An Idyll in Three Acts

(1937)

CHARACTERS

Francesca, aged 24
Cleofe, her aunt, aged 50
Alberto, aged 28
Ofelia, his aunt, aged 50
The Doctor, aged 30
Noemi, aged 25
Consalvo, aged 35
Adelaide, Cleofe's maid
A Commercial Traveller
A Postman
A Farmer

The time is the present day.

SUMMERTIME was produced at the Apollo Theatre, London, on November 9th, 1955, with the following cast:

FRANCESCA	GERALDINE MCEWAN
CLEOFE, her aunt	GWEN FFRANGCON DAVIES
ALBERTO	DIRK BOGARDE
OFELIA, his aunt	ESMA CANNON
THE DOCTOR	MICHAEL GWYNN
NOEMI	VIVIENNE DRUMMOND
CONSALVO	MARK DIGNAM
ADELAIDE, Cleofe's maid	MAUREEN QUINNEY
MARIA, Ofelia's maid	BARBARA NEW
A POSTMAN	TONY CHURCH
A FARMER	RONALD BARKER

The Play was produced by Peter Hall

The Scenery was designed by James Bailey

The Play was presented by Toby Rowland

ACT ONE

The scene is two small neighbouring gardens, attached to the cottages of MISS CLEOFE *and* MISS OFELIA. *They are separated by a fence of varnished wood, low enough to be easily stepped over. As is the fate of all elderly aunts living in the country, each of the ladies has her nephew or niece staying with her.*

MISS CLEOFE *is prowling about her garden, talking to her niece,* FRANCESCA, *who is quietly preparing and wrapping up sandwiches. The song of a number of caged canaries can be heard.*

CLEOFE: (*armed with spectacles, is counting the five apples on a dwarf apple tree near the fence.*) One. Two. Three. Four. Five. (*She counts them again.*) . . . Three. Four. *Five.* (*Indignantly*) I would just like to know who's had the sixth, that's all. It was here on this very tree last night.

FRANCESCA: Perhaps it was the milk boy, Aunt.

CLEOFE: (*who rarely pauses for breath*) Perhaps it was; I've never liked that boy. But it wouldn't surprise *me* very much if someone else had taken a fancy to it. It's not the apple I mind about, though of course it had to be the very best one on the tree. It's the principle of the thing. You might *think*, considering what close friends we've all been all these years, in and out of each other's houses all day long, *you might think* he'd have had the common decency to *ask* for the apple. Do you know what I'd have done? I'd have picked all six of them for him! Not just the one, all six: and I'd have sent them round to him, done up properly, in a nice little basket. Wouldn't I?

FRANCESCA: Yes, Aunt Cleofe, you would.

CLEOFE: (*unwearied*) Or we could have taken them with us on the picnic today, and eaten them up there, all together. Friendship is one thing, fruit's another. But, no. Every time the great Alberto comes here, you find there's an apple missing. It would be just the same if he had measles. When there aren't any apples, it's plums. Did you hear him last night? He can't even get home at a respectable hour now. And as thin as a rake. And it isn't just work in the city that makes him so thin. Did you hear him last night?

FRANCESCA: Yes, Aunt.

CLEOFE: I should just think so, he'd have woken a man in a trance. I don't know why anyone should have to make a row like that at night, when decent people are in bed asleep. And now, of course, *he's* asleep; and leaving us to do the work. He kindly condescends to come on the picnic with us; but who has to do the sandwiches? We do. What do you think he'd say if *I* started to whistle about the place, and race about the garden, and bang all the heavy furniture about in the middle of the night? I still can't think what he was doing. There was something very odd going on.

FRANCESCA: Perhaps he was just feeling happy, Aunt Cleofe.

CLEOFE: Well, I'm happy, too, sometimes. You never hear me whistle, do you? And there's another thing I don't approve of. (*Intensely*) How can he *lower* himself to stride over the fence? What's the garden gate there for?

FRANCESCA: He does it because it's quicker.

CLEOFE: I dare say. But it's the principle of the thing. It's rude; it's slovenly. In my day I'm glad to think we had a little more style. I suppose he thinks now they've offered him all these fine jobs in the city, he's above our poor little garden gate! In any case, I don't believe in all these jobs they keep talking about. They've been asking for him, and waiting for him, and I don't know what, for the last two months. Well, he can go as soon as he likes for all I care. He can go tomorrow, if he wants to. Did you say something?

FRANCESCA: No, Aunt.

CLEOFE: Are you sorry he's going?

FRANCESCA: But, Aunt, they only said he *might* be going.

CLEOFE: His aunt talks of nothing else, all day long: Alberto's splendid new job! Oh, she's not a bad woman, I'm not saying she is. But she never stops talking! She's a know-all. As well anyone might be who spends the whole day behind the shutters peering into what's going on in other people's houses through her late brother's *celebrated marine binoculars*. Not a very dignified thing to do, I would have thought.

FRANCESCA: (*warning*) Shhh!

CLEOFE: What's the matter?

FRANCESCA: (*nodding towards the other garden*) How very odd. I can hear tapping.

CLEOFE: Good heavens, you'd think they were knocking nails in.

FRANCESCA: There's someone in Alberto's room!

CLEOFE: Well, what did I tell you! Showing off. We're down here getting the picnic things ready, we leave in half an hour, and they can't even nod to us from the window. Your great Alberto . . .

FRANCESCA: Oh, but he'll be here presently, Aunt.

CLEOFE: I know he will. The minute he smells my tarts he'll be out like a shot, you can be sure of that.

FRANCESCA: But his aunt will have made some tarts, too, Aunt.

CLEOFE: There are tarts and tarts, my dear Francesca. The fact remains that every year we go on this wonderful picnic; we take our tarts, they take their tarts; which tarts come back? Theirs. There must be some reason for it, I suppose. Never so much as a *flake* of mine do you see brought back. (*Calls off, elaborately*) Adelaide! Isn't it about time you were taking the tartlets out of the oven?

ADELAIDE: (*off*) I'm just taking them out, Miss Cleofe.

CLEOFE: (*loudly*) And don't forget to grease them well, will you?

ADELAIDE: I'm just greasing them now, Miss Cleofe.

CLEOFE: Thank you! The truth of the matter *is*: your precious Alberto eats more of my tarts than all the rest of us put together. It surprises me he never gets stomach ache. It makes you think the meals he gets in the city must be barely enough to keep him going, in spite of all these wonderful *posts*. Do you know what *I* think, Francesca? I don't believe all this nonsense about big jobs in the city. I've seen too many people end up in the gutter. Even in jail sometimes.

FRANCESCA: Oh, do let's hope not, Aunt Cleofe.

CLEOFE: Let's hope not. But you know what happens in these big cities: bad companions, bad habits . . . and (*dropping her voice*) women. Alberto is the sort of lad who's *designed* for trouble, you can see it in his face. Would you call Alberto a *bright* young man?

FRANCESCA: Well . . . not altogether perhaps.

CLEOFE: I have no wish to compare him with the doctor. I'm not speaking of his education, of course. That's not his fault, it's the way they're taught nowadays. But, if you ask me, the trouble is Fibre. That's what it all comes down to. Fibre. Alberto's a good boy, no doubt, but he has no Fibre. You wouldn't say there's anything very splendid or remarkable about Alberto, would you?

FRANCESCA: Oh, no, he's just a good, nice boy, that's all.

CLEOFE: Ah! In my day a man was expected to appeal to a woman's imagination. A woman's heart. We insisted on it. A man had to *have* something! He even had to be . . . a bit of a scamp. (*Reminiscently*) My word, yes.

FRANCESCA: I don't think there's anything unpleasant about Alberto.

CLEOFE: No, you can't even say that for him. He isn't clever, he isn't handsome, he isn't rich, he has no Fibre. And we can't even pretend he's unpleasant.

FRANCESCA: (*without raising her eyes*) But, Auntie, you've said yourself . . .

CLEOFE: Yes, yes, I like him, I know. I'm not made of flint. I've seen him grow up. He's a good lad . . . (*She breaks off. She has noticed something unusual going on next door, off stage.*) That's very strange.

FRANCESCA: What is, Aunt?

CLEOFE: Their maid's just gone out. I could have

sworn she'd got letters to post. I saw them in her hand. And they're still knocking those nails in.

FRANCESCA: I wonder what's the matter.

CLEOFE: Well, what should be the matter? They're just very important people, that's all. And, in the meantime, *we* have to get on with cutting up sandwiches! (*Calls*) Adelaide! How have those tartlets turned out? Have they risen?

ADELAIDE: (*off*) Most of them, Miss Cleofe. Most of them have.

CLEOFE: As soon as you've greased them, bring them out here with some wrapping-up paper, will you?

ADELAIDE: Yes, Miss Cleofe.

CLEOFE: (*with a change of tone*) Francesca.

FRANCESCA: Yes, Aunt.

CLEOFE: You look very nice in that jacket.

FRANCESCA: I put it on for the picnic.

CLEOFE: You've grown into a fine girl, Francesca. It seems only yesterday you were in pinafores. (*Pause.*) I think it's about time you were thinking of getting married, Francesca.

FRANCESCA: *I've* no objection, Aunt.

CLEOFE: All your friends are getting engaged and married. (*Drops her voice a little*) Francesca, last night after you'd gone out the doctor was talking to me again. Oh, nothing unusual . . . but you wouldn't have to be a mind reader to see that he'd be very glad to marry you. He's a man with very fine qualities, the doctor.

FRANCESCA: Don't you think he's rather a bore?

CLEOFE: So a husband should be. When husbands are entertaining you very soon find it's not their wives they entertain. It's other women. The doctor's a fine figure of a man. Nice voice. Manly. Well-bred. Got on very well in his profession. And quite well off. A woman would find him a great comfort about the place.

FRANCESCA: I don't like the way the doctor does his hair.

CLEOFE: Francesca, you're not a child any longer. The doctor's just the sort of man who makes a woman really happy. His brother, the one who married the eldest Maes girl, takes her up a pot of coffee and two boiled eggs in bed every morning. I know it for a fact. That's what I call a husband. A man who runs and gets something to put round his wife's shoulders the minute it begins to get chilly.

FRANCESCA: But, Aunt, if I were married, *I* should be the one who wanted to take my husband *his* breakfast in bed, and put something round his shoulders when it got chilly.

CLEOFE: My dear Francesca, I've a horrible fear you're the kind of girl who's fated to get herself made a *victim* of.

FRANCESCA: Oh, I hope not, Aunt Cleofe.

CLEOFE: Francesca.

FRANCESCA: Yes, Aunt.

CLEOFE: Everyone knows you're in love with Alberto. A blind man could see it.

FRANCESCA: (*calmly, as though it were unimportant*) I like him.

CLEOFE: Head over heels, I should have said. More's the pity. And what are you going to do about it, may I ask?

FRANCESCA: (*as before*) I'd like to marry him.

CLEOFE: Oh. Well, you seem fairly clear on the point. What about him. What does he say?

FRANCESCA: Nothing.

CLEOFE: What do you mean: nothing?

FRANCESCA: (*calmly*) I don't think he's noticed.

CLEOFE: (*staggered*) Alberto's *never noticed* you're madly in love with him?

FRANCESCA: I don't think so, Aunt.

CLEOFE: Are you sure he's not pretending? Men are very crafty.

FRANCESCA: No, I really don't think so.

CLEOFE: God bless my soul. What a ... *turnip*! Young men were very different in my day. They were ... full of ardour. But, my dear child, haven't you tried ... in any way ... to *show* him what you feel?

FRANCESCA: Well, you can imagine, Aunt.

CLEOFE: Yes, I can imagine. Perfectly well. I only asked as a formality. And Alberto still ...

FRANCESCA: Nothing.

CLEOFE: (*indignantly*) And what do you intend to do about it?

FRANCESCA: (*calmly*) I intend to marry him, Aunt.

CLEOFE: But doesn't it make your blood boil to think he never notices you?

FRANCESCA: (*calmly*) I could punch his head.

CLEOFE: ... when there are lots of young men who are falling over each other just to look at you.

FRANCESCA: It's because we've grown up together, you see, Aunt. He still thinks I'm just a boy friend, in spite of my skirts.

CLEOFE: Boy friend! Doesn't he ever wonder why you haven't done your military service?

FRANCESCA: A boy friend, that's how he sees me. It can't be helped.

CLEOFE: And how is it you don't think of him as a girl friend in trousers?

FRANCESCA: (*resigned*) I think it must all have begun when I was very little. Whenever I used to play at being a lady I had to have a gentleman, and as there were no other boys except Alberto about the place, it always had to be Alberto.

CLEOFE: Is that how it was?

FRANCESCA: Yes, that was it. (*Wistfully*) Aunt, do you remember when poor Uncle Venturino had gallstones, and he said it used to give him a terrible pain right deep down? Well, that's how I feel whenever I think of Alberto marrying anyone else.

CLEOFE: Your uncle always exaggerated everything, of course. Francesca, my dear, *I* wasn't such a bad-looking girl, when I was young. *I also* used to go with young gentlemen on picnics up in the mountains just like we do now. And look at me. I'm just an old parrot now, that's all. Time races on, Francesca. You mustn't let it slip past you like this.

FRANCESCA: But I don't want it to slip past, Auntie.

CLEOFE: I'm quite sure if I'd been in your place, I'd have seen to it that . . . some little thing or other happened, to make him *do* something. Oh, something quite innocent, I mean, of course.

FRANCESCA: (*in a low voice*) I do think up things sometimes. For example, I sometimes imagine . . . you won't laugh at me, will you?

CLEOFE: I may even envy you, my dear.

FRANCESCA: I imagine that I've had some great

sorrow or other. For example, a death in the family, perhaps . . .

CLEOFE: Let's hope there'll still be time for that.

FRANCESCA: A death in the family—and I'm standing there crying, just by the apple tree. And suddenly Alberto comes out . . .

CLEOFE: (*resignedly*) Striding over the fence, no doubt.

FRANCESCA: And he comes up to me to comfort me. And then I throw myself sobbing on his chest.

CLEOFE: (*doubtfully*) Yes, well, he *might* give you a little squeeze, I dare say. That wouldn't get you very far.

FRANCESCA: (*shyly*) Once something did happen rather like that. I'd been frightened. By a lizard.

CLEOFE: (*curious rather than severe*) And you actually threw yourself on his chest?

FRANCESCA: Yes.

CLEOFE: What did he do?

FRANCESCA: He put his hand here.

CLEOFE: (*interested*) On his heart?

FRANCESCA: No, on his fountain pen. He was afraid I'd broken it.

CLEOFE: Bah! (*Sympathetically*) My poor Francesca . . . I shouldn't be a woman if I didn't understand. (*In sudden surprise, looking off-stage*) Good gracious! What on earth are they doing with rope?

FRANCESCA: Rope?

CLEOFE: Their maid has just gone in again with a coil of rope.

FRANCESCA: And they haven't even watered the flowers this morning.

CLEOFE: There's something going on. I can sense it. (*Raising her voice and evidently greeting her neighbour*) Good morning, Miss Ofelia!

OFELIA: (*off-stage, as from a window, in busy tones*) Good morning, good morning! Have you heard? Wonderful news! Great news for Alberto! I'll be with you in a jiffy!

A pause. Evidently OFELIA *has withdrawn from the window.*

CLEOFE: Now, there's nothing to worry about, Francesca. My dear child, you've gone quite pale. "Good news for Alberto!" Such nonsense. Never you mind, my dear. (*A pause. Then she speaks in a new, resolute, almost masculine tone.*) Francesca.

FRANCESCA: Yes, Aunt.

CLEOFE: Officially, Francesca, I ought to be against all this. But, privately speaking, I'm dying to help you. We must make up our minds at once.

FRANCESCA: About what, Aunt?

CLEOFE: We must act. There's no time to lose. He may be leaving any minute. The world is full of shameless women. They'll snap him up and marry him, and all you'll get is the news.

FRANCESCA: What do you think I ought to do?

CLEOFE: Bring him to the point. Today. Up there. At the picnic. It may be only a matter of hours, Francesca. Why don't you try and make him jealous of the doctor? While we're all up there? Or better still: sprain your ankle. It's quite usual. It's often done. He'll be forced to pick you up and carry you. And after that the . . . well, the rest will be up to you.

FRANCESCA: (*doubtfully*) But, Aunt, you see that sort of thing the whole time at the pictures. (*Dropping her eyes*) And in any case, Aunt Cleofe, I . . . I've thought of something else. Another way.

CLEOFE: You've thought of one already?

FRANCESCA: Yes.

CLEOFE: What way?

FRANCESCA: (*calmly*) I shall tell him.

CLEOFE: Tell him?

FRANCESCA: Yes.

CLEOFE: (*alarmed*) Tell him what?

FRANCESCA: Everything.

CLEOFE: (*after a pause—alarmed*) What, straight out? Today?

FRANCESCA: Yes, Aunt.

CLEOFE: You'll propose to him—yourself!

FRANCESCA: I think . . . it's probably safer that way.

CLEOFE: (*after a pause—with admiration*) Francesca, if I'd been a man, I'd like to have married you myself.

OFELIA *enters*.

OFELIA: Good morning, everybody. Good morning.

CLEOFE: }
FRANCESCA: } Good morning.

OFELIA: (*importantly*) Girls, I'm covered with dust. Literally.

CLEOFE: (*indifferently*) Anything happened?

OFELIA (*triumphantly*) Happened! He's leaving!

CLEOFE: Leaving? Who is?

OFELIA: Alberto, of course! To take up his new post. They want him at once.

CLEOFE: (*contemptuously*) Who does?

OFELIA: (*rather piqued*) The bank.

CLEOFE: (*aggressively*) Whatever for?

OFELIA: What for! Why, he's being given a confidential post.

CLEOFE: What's he going to do with it?

OFELIA: Well . . . he'll . . . *run* things.

CLEOFE: (*sourly*) Run a bank?

OFELIA: I didn't say that. But they certainly want him for a very important post. (*Dropping her voice*) He'll have a room to himself.

CLEOFE: (*a little taken aback*) We've been hearing about that room to himself for the last two months. When's he going?

OFELIA: Why, immediately, my dear. Today. Tomorrow. I don't know quite. You know what these banks are. Everything's a matter of urgency.

FRANCESCA: (*a little unsteadily*) But . . . what about the picnic this afternoon? W-won't Alberto be able to come to the picnic?

OFELIA: Why, my dear, I can't say. I shouldn't think so. It's a big change in his life, this is, you know.

CLEOFE: (*very angry*) You mean, he's not coming to the picnic?

OFELIA: I'm afraid not. I'm so sorry.

CLEOFE: And you wait till *now* to come and tell us!

OFELIA: I'm sorry, my dear. I've been making tarts for it, too. But we've much too much to do, girls. I'm sure you understand.

FRANCESCA: (*faintly*) But . . . won't he even come to say goodbye to us? And talk to us a bit?

OFELIA: Well, he's terribly busy, poor boy. But, oh,

of course, he'll come and say goodbye. Just for a minute, last thing tonight.

Pause.

CLEOFE: Ah. Just for a minute. Last thing tonight. We'll see about that. (*Calls solemnly*) Adelaide! Bring the tartlets out here.

ADELAIDE: (*off*) I was just bringing them, Miss Cleofe. (*She enters, bearing a wooden dish, laden with tarts.*)

CLEOFE: Just put them down over there; where they can be seen.

ADELAIDE *deposits the dish on a low bench and retreats.*

OFELIA: Oh, how lovely, how lovely. What a lovely, lovely smell! Clever Adelaide.

CLEOFE: Clever Francesca, you mean. She measured all the ingredients out herself. You don't find many girls like Francesca these days.

ALBERTO *enters, in shirt sleeves, and strides across the fence.*

ALBERTO: (*as he enters*) Good morning, everyone. What a lovely smell!

CLEOFE: (*drily*) Good morning.

FRANCESCA: Hello, Alberto.

ALBERTO: Hello. Have you all heard? The bank has sent for us at last. The main branch.

CLEOFE: Let's hope it doesn't snap off.

ALBERTO: (*his eyes on the tarts*) No. We shall be there, Aunt Cleofe. Eyes like a lynx and wrists of steel.

CLEOFE: And plenty of lick . . . I trust.

ALBERTO: Lick?

CLEOFE: For sticking down envelopes.

OFELIA: (*hurt*) Oh, but Alberto's going to have tremendous great offices.

ALBERTO: (*detaching a piece of crust from one of the tarts and eating it*) Sorry, Aunt Cleofe, I was just taking a crumb of one of your tarts. It was flaking off. The truth is, these wily old bankers know what they're doing.

OFELIA: They understand. They know how to appreciate the right people.

ALBERTO: Whoever would have thought that ... sorry, Aunt Cleofe, I might as well have this little bit, mightn't I? It was flaking off. Lovely. I was saying, whoever would have thought they'd had their eyes on me all this time.

OFELIA: You're too modest, Albert. That's your trouble.

FRANCESCA has meanwhile been bringing up a basket chair. ALBERTO sinks into it.

ALBERTO: Auff! I've done nothing but strap up suitcases all morning. I'm worn out. I'm all for the simple life myself. All these important jobs—rushing around the whole time. I get fed up with it, you know.

OFELIA: There. That's your modesty again.

ALBERTO: (*detaching another piece of crust from the tarts, which Francesca has thoughtfully placed beside him*) I say, Aunt Cleofe, these tarts really are marvellous. They melt in the mouth.

CLEOFE: So it would seem. Help yourself. And *I'm* not your aunt. That's your aunt.

ALBERTO: (*mouth full*) Do you know what I've been thinking? I've been thinking all morning about how I've got to leave you, Aunt Cleofe and Francesca. And

Aunt Ofelia, too, of course, only she'll be joining me in the city later on . . . But when I thought of it all, do you know, I felt something dreadful *here*? My stomach seemed to close right up.

CLEOFE: (*with a glance at him*) One would hardly have thought so.

ALBERTO: (*nostalgically*) What memories! What wonderful years! It seems only yesterday we first came here for the holidays. Do you remember, Aunt Cleofe, when I broke that branch? The branch of the old pear tree.

CLEOFE: Yes. And poor little Francesca took all the blame herself, as usual, to get you out of it. And you let her be smacked for it.

OFELIA: Yes, but he was very young at the time.

CLEOFE: Well, wasn't Francesca? She was younger than he was. She always has been. And she let them smack her without a whimper. For *you*, Alberto. Ah, Francesca's got you out of a lot of trouble before now.

ALBERTO: (*mouth full*) Wonderful times. I'll send you a new pear tree, Aunt Cleofe, shall I? From the city. A present. A Japanese pear tree. Have you ever seen one? It's a pear tree that looks like an apple tree. It has apple blossom, and it grows lovely apples on it. It's exactly like an apple tree. Only it's a pear. It's Japanese. And a watering can. I'll send you one of those with a pump. The sort you squirt.

CLEOFE (*suspiciously*) A watering can?

ALBERTO: Yes. Yours must have got a bit dented in. Last night. It got under my foot . . . And the fuchsias as well. I'll see to all that.

CLEOFE: (*alarmed*) My fuchsias?

ALBERTO: (*his mouth still full*) Yes. I told you: the watering can tripped me up. I think I must have landed up in the fuchsia-bed. (*He breaks off; he has been fumbling beneath himself for something, and now produces a pair of spectacles.*) Oh, Aunt Cleofe, now that *is* your fault. You really shouldn't leave your glasses about the place like that.

CLEOFE: (*with resigned fury*) You've sat on my spectacles. You haven't broken anything else, I suppose, by any chance?

ALBERTO: Come, come, Aunt Cleofe, don't be cross. (*Coaxing*) Forget and forgive, m'm? *Yes*. It may be a very long time before I break anything else of yours, after all. I'll send you a whole great pile of presents from the city. And to Francesca, too: I'll send cartloads of them. Shall I, Francesca?

CLEOFE: "Shall I, Francesca?" Yes, we know. She'll soon get tired of looking out for *them*. Her big day has arrived, too. She'll be getting married very shortly.

ALBERTO: Francesca?

CLEOFE: Yes, Francesca. She's a lovely girl. Everyone says so. Of course, she'll be getting married.

ALBERTO: (*not very pleased*) I . . . I don't see what that's got to do with anything . . . Surely, it's a bit premature, isn't it? Francesca's still . . . well, I mean, she's still . . . so undeveloped.

CLEOFE: (*coldly*) Well, some we could name don't seem to think so.

OFELIA: Oh, Cleofe, *really*, Is that so? How lovely? Is there really something . . . brewing?

CLEOFE: (*sharply*) Brewing?

OFELIA: Well . . . you know.

Francesca: (*embarrassed*) I wish there were!

Ofelia: Oh, I see. You mean it's all rather vague at the moment?

Cleofe: (*dignified*) Vague, *perhaps* . . . up to a point.

Ofelia: Oh, how *splendid*, how lovely. How lovely, how splendid.

Alberto: (*not quite sure why all this displeases him*) Well, *I* think it's all rather . . . I dunno. It seems to me . . . well a bit *silly* for Francesca to be in such a hurry.

Francesca: Of course, it is. I agree with you, Alberto.

Cleofe: (*severely*) There is no question of hurry. It's simply that time is not standing still. There is a time for pears, apples, watering cans. But, in the meanwhile, some people are growing up, even if others aren't.

Alberto: (*crossly*) What on earth have you put in these tarts, Aunt Cleofe? Oh, I mean, they're very nice, but goodness me, they do seem to stick . . . just here. (*He touches his throat.*)

Francesca: (*solicitously*) I've made you some coffee, Alberto. You know, the way you like it.

Cleofe: (*not to be sidetracked*) Francesca has grown up into a splendid young woman.

Ofelia: That new jacket looks very nice on you, Francesca.

Francesca: Oh, thank you. Do *you* like it, Alberto?

Alberto: (*not very cheerful*) M'm? Yes, it's all right. I mean, yes, it looks very nice.

Francesca: (*with a note of pleading*) Alberto, surely you're not going to stay away from the picnic this afternoon? We've been every year.

OFELIA: I wish we could, my dear. But, alas. We have things to see to. Excuse me, my dears. Don't stay there dawdling, Alberto. (*She goes out.*)

ALBERTO: I shan't be long, Auntie. (*Drinking the coffee Francesca has brought him*) It's been jolly nice here anyway. Ah, the life I've got to face won't be all sugar and spice. Struggles. Hard times. City life . . . It gets you down; wears you out; turns you upside down. Cold little lodgings; stale air; restaurant food the whole time. And all the frightful dirt.

FRANCESCA: Alberto, we're going to take the spirit lamp with us. After lunch we could have a little grog, with pineapple.

ALBERTO: Hot?

FRANCESCA: Of course. It'll be lovely. And the air's so fresh up there, too. It'll do you good. You look rather tired.

CLEOFE: (*diplomatically*) It could hardly be a better day for it, all things considered.

FRANCESCA: It'll be your last day with us. Do you remember it up there? The lovely meadows; all those blue flowers? . . . You'll be glad to look back on it later. And we can talk about . . . all sorts of things.

The ancient POSTMAN *of the locality has appeared on the road, during these remarks.*

THE POSTMAN: Excuse me.

CLEOFE: Come in.

THE POSTMAN: (*solemnly*) Good morning, each. There's a telegram. It's for you, Mr. Alberto.

ALBERTO: (*with casual grandeur*) Telegrams, you see. *They're* beginning now. I thought as much. Thank you.

Now, I wonder who on earth it can be from. (*He tears it open and stares at it blankly. There is a pause.*)

CLEOFE: Is it from the bank?

ALBERTO: (*baffled*) No.

FRANCESCA: Good news?

ALBERTO: It seems to be from somebody called ... (*reading*) ... Miani. (*Thinking*) Miani? (*Shrugging*) But *I* don't know anyone called Miani.

CLEOFE: Is it a mistake?

ALBERTO: Well, it's very odd. It says: (*he reads aloud slowly*) "CONSALVO COMING SEE YOU TOMORROW STOP." Consalvo? I don't know anyone called Consalvo. And why should he be coming to see me?

CLEOFE: Is that all it says?

ALBERTO: No, it says: "DON'T WORRY STOP BE VERY CAREFUL STOP SHALL ALSO BE THERE MYSELF TO GIVE YOU HELL, MIANI". Who *is* Miani? I don't know who he is. And why ... why should he want to GIVE ME HELL?

THE POSTMAN: (*knowledgeably*) No, Mr. Alberto. That reads: "GIVE YOU HELP".

ALBERTO: Oh, I see. Well, that's better. (*Rather worried*) But why do they tell me DON'T WORRY STOP BE VERY CAREFUL STOP, I wonder? It must be a joke.

THE POSTMAN: (*gloomily*) Let's hope so, Mr. Alberto. I've delivered a lot of them things in my time, and they don't always bode good. Good morning, each. (*He retreats.*)

THE OTHERS: (*rather startled*) Good morning.

ALBERTO: DON'T WORRY STOP BE VERY CAREFUL STOP. But why *should* I worry? (*Worried*) I ... I mean, why should I?

CLEOFE: Alberto. This couldn't be another of your celebrated *scrapes*, I suppose?

ALBERTO: No, no, Aunt Cleofe, really it isn't. I simply don't know who Consalvo and Miani are at all. (*Rather indignant*) And I'd really like to know why a . . . a city man like myself, a business man, has to be exposed to this . . . this sort of . . . (*breaks off.*)

THE POSTMAN: (*returning*) Excuse me, Mr. Alberto, did I give you two or only one? Telegrams, I mean.

ALBERTO: Only one. This one.

THE POSTMAN: There should have been two. Where is it? (*He is searching in his pockets.*) I know I put it somewhere. (*Crossly*) The number of people who keep getting telegrams these days, you wouldn't think. It wasn't like this in the old days. Ah. I knew I'd got it. There.

ALBERTO: Give it to me. (*He opens it, hastily, and reads it. There is a long silence.*) This . . . this is from Consalvo.

THE POSTMAN: (*to the women*) He says he's coming tomorrow.

ALBERTO: (*reads*) It says: "COMPLETE EXPLANATION REQUIRED STOP FACTS KNOWN STOP." Facts known stop—what does that mean? "KINDLY EXPECT ME TOMORROW STOP GUIDO CONSALVO NICOLA BENEDÈ." (*Pause.*) Damn it, I can't . . . Guido, Consalvo, Nicola . . . I can't even tell you how many there are of them. And why are they coming here? It's . . . it's outrageous. (*Optimistically*) Oh, it must be a mistake.

CLEOFE: (*severely*) Oh, yes, of course; you're not the sort of person who . . .

ALBERTO: But no, Aunt Cleofe, I swear I . . .

CLEOFE: . . . goes from one mess smack into another, are you?

ALBERTO: (*reading*) FACTS KNOWN STOP.

CLEOFE: I cxpect they are. It's just what might have been expected from the life you've been leading these last few months.

FRANCESCA: (*reproachfully*) Aunt!

CLEOFE: Well, well, it's very, very easy to take a wrong turning.

ALBERTO: But, Aunt Cleofe, I swear to you there's *been* no wrong turning. I don't know what "facts known" means. I'm quite innocent. (*With a change of tone*) I think it must be some madman.

CLEOFE: (*gravely, shaking her head*) Alberto, my dear boy, we know you.

ALBERTO: "KINDLY EXPECT ME TOMORROW," it says, "STOP." Tomorrow? (*He laughs slightly, suddenly relieved.*) Well, the poor things. They want me to expect them tomorrow. The poor old things. Tomorrow, I shan't be here to expect anyone. I shall be far away; a mere drop in the great ocean of the metropolis. Poor Consalvo . . . it's a pity. It's sad to think of him coming all the way here for nothing, whoever he is. (*Confidently*) And time will spread its kindly mantle of forgetfulness over the whole thing. I . . . I suppose.

THE POSTMAN: (*genuinely distressed*) Mr. Alberto, I'm very, very sorry, but our office shuts at seven in the evening.

ALBERTO: (*cheerfully*) Does it? I'm very glad to hear it.

THE POSTMAN: (*apologetically*) What I mean is the telegrams that come after seven we don't get them till the day after. That's to say, the following morning, I mean.

ALBERTO: (*loftily*) And what's all that to do with me?

THE POSTMAN: Well, that's why your telegrams, instead of you getting them last night . . .

ALBERTO: (*anxiously*) . . . last night?

THE POSTMAN: You've had 'em today; that's to say . . .

ALBERTO: (*staring before him*) . . . the following morning.

THE POSTMAN: Yes, Mr. Alberto. It says tomorrow . . . and it *was* tomorrow, yesterday. But it's today, today.

ALBERTO: (*who at last understands*) I see. Damn. (*A pause: he looks at the telegrams; then, instinctively, at the highroad: to* CLEOFE.) Did . . . did you follow that?

CLEOFE: Throughout.

ALBERTO: (*apprehensively*) It means . . . Consalvo may be here . . . any moment. I . . . (*He pauses—then, clutching at a hope.*) Oh, I'm sure it's just a joke.

The POSTMAN *has gone out of the gate; as he closes it, a well-dressed* STRANGER *appears on the highroad at the back of the stage.*

THE STRANGER: (*in a business-like voice*) Good morning. Have I the honour of addressing Mr. Alberto Moesse?

ALBERTO: No.

CLEOFE: Yes.

ALBERTO: Yes, I mean. I . . . I'm Moesse.

THE POSTMAN: (*funereally*) Good morning, each. (*He departs.*)

THE STRANGER: (*advancing briskly*) Good morning. I was given your address by the District Councillor, a most obliging gentleman.

ALBERTO: What . . . what is it you want?

THE STRANGER: It is not the first time that the District Councillor has given me his confidence. (*Brightly*) Mr. Moesse! May I draw your attention to *this*? (*He has drawn a small box from his trouser pocket, with a sudden gesture that terrifies Alberto and makes the two women start.*)

ALBERTO: Are you Consalvo?

THE STRANGER: (*surprised*) No, sir.

ALBERTO: Are you Miani?

THE STRANGER: (*disconcerted*) I'm Pakke.

ALBERTO: Pakke? What do you want me for?

THE STRANGER: (*nervously showing the object*) I . . . I'm travelling in fountain pens, sir. I . . .

ALBERTO: (*furiously*) Get out! How dare you! Leave me alone! Get out of here and go back where you came from!

THE STRANGER: (*rapidly withdrawing*) I'm going, sir. I'm so sorry. I'm going. (*He vanishes down the road.*)

ALBERTO: How can people have the impertinence to come marching into people's gardens like that, when . . . (*He breaks off. Pause.*) Oh. Oh, dear.

It is no longer the stranger whom ALBERTO *is troubled by. He is staring at the highroad, where an elegant young lady in travelling-clothes has appeared.*

NOEMI: (*approaching*) Good morning, Alberto.

ALBERTO: (*greatly baffled*) G-good morning. Hello, Noemi.

NOEMI: Am I in time? I raced here. What . . . whatever's the matter?

ALBERTO: I . . . I'm just surprised, that's all.

NOEMI: Surprised? didn't you get my telegram?

ALBERTO: No. Yes. I've had two. But . . . not one from you . . . I don't think. Here they are. (*He produces them.*)

NOEMI: Let me see. (*She scans them.*) You are a great silly, Alberto. They've written 'Miani'. It's Noemi. Surely you might have guessed that at least.

ALBERTO: Yes, yes, yes. I . . . I did almost guess. But I was hoping . . .

NOEMI: Is Consalvo here yet?

ALBERTO: (*in anguished tones*) But . . . but who *is* Consalvo?

NOEMI: You really are an idiot, Alberto! Look, I must talk to you. (*With a momentary glance at the others, who are watching in some perplexity*) Will you excuse us for a moment, please?

CLEOFE: (*frigidly*) With pleasure.

NOEMI: Come over here for a moment, Alberto, They've found out all about what . . .

She has energetically drawn him away from the others, whispering rapidly and intently. Nothing at first is heard of their conversation; then, after a moment or two, certain rather disturbing remarks are heard, louder than the rest of their murmured colloquy.

CLEOFE: I said it. I knew it. I sensed it.

NOEMI: (*her voice rising slightly*) . . . but I must warn you, darling, he's absolutely furious. He'll do anything.

ALBERTO: I refuse to see him. I'm quite innocent. You know I am . . .

They become inaudible again.

FRANCESCA: Oh, Aunt Cleofe, do you think anything serious has happened?

CLEOFE: What has happened was bound to happen. I sensed it.

NOEMI: (*louder*) . . . Can't you understand? He's like an absolute tiger when he's roused. And there'll be that trial as well.

ALBERTO: *Trial?*

NOEMI: Of course, there will. The whole thing's a disaster.

FRANCESCA: Oh, why did he ever have to get mixed up with city people?

CLEOFE: I knew it. I sensed it.

NOEMI: He'll certainly prosecute. He isn't joking, he means what he says . . .

ALBERTO: . . . trying to pretend I'm a criminal now! Is that what he thinks?

NOEMI: (*concluding*) He'll be here any minute. There's no time to lose. Try and think what you're going to say to him. I'll go and watch on the road.

She goes to the back of the stage and watches the road.

ALBERTO: Thank you. Yes, do. I . . . one moment, Aunt Cleofe, Francesca.

CLEOFE: I sensed it.

ALBERTO: I must just think for a minute. I . . . (*After a brief pause*) Look, I *will* come to the picnic with you Francesca and Aunt Cleofe. It will do no good. I . . . the fresh air. I'll be ready in half a minute, and we can start at once. (*A pleading whisper*) Francesca, I must get away from these people as soon as possible. I'll explain later. (*Louder*) We'll take Aunt Ofelia, too. It'll be best.

Then we can shut up the house and everything'll be all right. (*He calls to* NOEMI) Excuse me a minute, Noemi, I'm just going indoors for a moment.

NOEMI: (*from back*) All right, darling.

ALBERTO *leaps across the fence, and disappears.*

FRANCESCA: (*continuing to assemble things for the picnic*) Good morning, Noemi.

NOEMI: (*surprised*) Oh! Francesca! It's you! *You're* here.

FRANCESCA: (*calmly*) So it seems.

NOEMI: I didn't notice who it was. Well, well, what a strange mix-up. What a small world it is!

FRANCESCA: Aunt, this is Mrs. . . . it *is* Mrs. . . . isn't it, now, Noemi?

NOEMI: It *was*, dear. I'm a widow now. Mrs. Noemi Bata.

CLEOFE: (*coldly*) How do you do?

FRANCESCA: Noemi was my rival for top place at school.

NOEMI: (*laughing*) Oh yes, we hated each other.

CLEOFE: You'll pardon me if I appear to leave you for a moment, won't you? (*She departs.*)

NOEMI: But, you know, you're still very pretty, my dear. Enchanting.

FRANCESCA: (*bitter-sweetly*) Oh, but so are you, Noemi. Even now.

NOEMI: (*bitter-sweetly*) You're still not married?

FRANCESCA: No, dear, not yet.

NOEMI: A nice young man, your next-door neighbour.

FRANCESCA: (*politely*) I suppose he is, yes. I've never noticed. (*With an evident hint of sarcasm*) I suppose you must have met him at the seaside somewhere? On the beach?

NOEMI: Yes, dear. (*With gentle spitefulness*) Darling, you know you really ought to put your hair up. You'd look much better. Not quite so . . . well, not quite so countrified, you know.

FRANCESCA: Thank you, I'll think about it.

The noise of a motor-horn is heard. An ancient motor-car appears on the road. It is driven by the DOCTOR.

THE DOCTOR: (*speaking from the motor-car. He is archly ceremonious in manner and determined at all costs to be gallant and playful.*) Here we are! Here we are! Here we *are*! (*Getting out, and coming into the garden*) Good morning, good morning, fair ladies. I would be very sorry to be late for such an occasion. But, here I am. The mountains await us.

FRANCESCA: We are ready, Doctor.

THE DOCTOR: (*gallantly*) Ah, more radiant than ever today, Miss Francesca. A veritable springtime floweret.

ALBERTO: (*off-stage, calling from a window*) We're coming at once, Doctor! Keep the engine running.

NOEMI: Are you going on an outing, Francesca?

FRANCESCA: (*coldly*) Yes, a picnic.

NOEMI: Oh, how sweet.

FRANCESCA: I'm so sorry I can't ask you to come with us. But, of course, we've made all the arrangements now—the food and so on.

NOEMI: Oh, of course, my dear. (*She retires to keep watch on the road.*)

CLEOFE: (*entering, followed by* ADELAIDE *with packages*

and baskets) Come on. Are we all ready? Bring those things to the motor, Adelaide. Good morning. Doctor.

THE DOCTOR: Good morning, dear lady.

CLEOFE: Hurry up, Francesca. Shall I sit next to you, Doctor?

THE DOCTOR: (*helping her in*) Mount, dear lady. The barometer points to dry. A light clouding over to the south-west, but inconsiderable in amount. I trust that my raincoat will prove quite superfluous. And likewise my little black bag, the doctor's friend.

CLEOFE: What on earth have you brought your little black bag for?

THE DOCTOR: Prudence is never a vice, dear lady. You might fall into some deep ravine.

CLEOFE: No, I shan't.

THE DOCTOR: And are you not bringing an umbrella? (*Musically*) One never can tell in the mountains—forewarned is forearmed. (*Coyly*) Have you never heard that before?

CLEOFE: Often.

OFELIA: (*hurrying on, armed with binoculars; she is not very well pleased.*) Oh dear, oh dear, what a dreadful muddle and confusion. First Alberto says one thing, then he says another. (*She climbs into the motor-car.*)

FRANCESCA: (*calls*) Alberto!

ALBERTO: (*off*) Coming!

OFELIA: (*a loud singing call*) Alberto! Albertino! Close the door of the drawing room!

ALBERTO: (*off*) I'm closing it!

They are now all in the car, except FRANCESCA, *who has remained in the garden, waiting for* ALBERTO. *Suddenly*

NOEMI, *in a state of alarm, runs from the road over to* FRANCESCA.

NOEMI: (*in a whisper*) My God, here he is. Coming down the road.

FRANCESCA: Who?

NOEMI: Consalvo. I don't want him to find me here. Is there another way out?

FRANCESCA: No. But you can go and hide in that place over there. (*She indicates a little low door.*)

NOEMI: Thank you. He's terrible when he's angry.

FRANCESCA: (*pushing her towards the little door*) Quick. Go in there.

NOEMI: (*protesting*) But it's a henhouse!

FRANCESCA: Yes, dear. Go on. Good luck.

She pushes NOEMI *in, locks the door and gives a sigh of relief. She is hardly in time before* CONSALVO, *large, dark and threatening, appears on the road. He comes determinedly in through the gate. Simultaneously,* ALBERTO *enters precipitately, leaping over the fence, on his way to the car. The two men and* FRANCESCA *suddenly find themselves all face to face. They stop.*

CONSALVO: Does Mr. Alberto Moesse live here?

ALBERTO: (*rather frightened*) I ... don't ... (*To* FRANCESCA) D-does he live here?

FRANCESCA: (*calmly*) Yes, sir, he does live here.

CONSALVO: (*savagely*) I've got to speak to him. It's very urgent. I've been travelling ever since yesterday evening. Where is he?

FRANCESCA: (*with winning charm*) Are you Mr. Consalvo?

CONSALVO: Yes.

FRANCESCA: I think you sent a telegram?

CONSALVO: Yes.

FRANCESCA: Announcing that you were coming?

CONSALVO: Yes.

FRANCESCA: (*angelically*) Then Mr. Moesse must be at the station waiting for you.

CONSALVO: At the station?

FRANCESCA: Yes, surely.

CONSALVO: But he doesn't know me!

FRANCESCA: No, but he knows everyone else, and so he'd be bound to pick you out. You will be the only one he doesn't know, you see. This is a very small place, sir.

CONSALVO: Where is this station?

FRANCESCA: Take the main road, then to the right, then to the right again, and then ask. It's only about four miles.

ALBERTO: (*helpfully*) Less. About three and three-quarters.

FRANCESCA: (*sweetly, departing towards the car*) We must be going. Good morning, sir. (*To* ALBERTO, *hostilely*) Come on, you.

ALBERTO: (*to* CONSALVO *as he cheerfully moves towards the car*) Good morning, sir. Good morning.

The motor has begun to move, with much festive blowing of the horn. It disappears. CONSALVO *is about to go on his way, when his attention is drawn to a series of loud knocks from the inside of the henhouse.*

NOEMI: Let me out! Please, someone! Come and let me out!

CONSALVO *goes over to the door and throws it open.* NOEMI *emerges, angrily, pulling cobwebs from her dress.*

CONSALVO: (*astounded*) Noemi! What on earth were you doing in there?

NOEMI: (*angrily*) Never you mind! Where's that maid?

ADELAIDE: (*dully*) Yes, ma'am?

NOEMI: Where have they gone?

ADELAIDE: (*solemnly*) They've gone to the Madonna of the Mountain, ma'am.

NOEMI: (*angrily*) Have they indeed! Then *I'm* going to the Madonna of the Mountain, too! (*She rushes out of the gate and after the car.*)

CONSALVO: (*who has stood there, dazed, pulls himself quickly together and shouts*) Are you! Then, by God, *I'm* going to the Madonna of the Mountain as well!

He is rushing off after NOEMI *as the* CURTAIN FALLS.

ACT TWO

An alpine spot not far from the Madonna of the Mountain. On one side of the stage there is an abandoned hut, an alpine refuge; on the other side is suggested a cliff that drops almost straight down. A little over an hour has gone by. The occasional barking of dogs is heard off stage. FRANCESCA *and the* DOCTOR *burst on to the scene, carrying baskets and bags.*

FRANCESCA: Here we are then, Doctor: here at last. (*She turns and calls—evidently to others of the party*) Oohoo! Oohoo! . . .

VOICES: (*very far away*) Oohoo . . . oohoo . . . !

ALBERTO: (*approaching, heavily laden, and in a bad temper*) Yes: oohoo, oohoo! I've never come up here by a worse path in my life before. (*To* FRANCESCA, *who ostentatiously takes no notice of him*) I'd like to know why on earth you've made us come here? Why couldn't we have gone with the others? They're already there. Look. You can see them. They're at the chapel already. Was the picnic supposed to be at the Madonna of the Mountain, or wasn't it? Why have you brought us here? Bullying everyone as usual.

THE DOCTOR: Oh, come—come—come. Come, come. Come.

FRANCESCA: (*sharply*) You could have stayed behind, couldn't you? Why didn't you stay and look after your visitors? (*To the* DOCTOR, *with extreme kindness*) Do you like it here, Doctor?

THE DOCTOR: (*enraptured*) Enchanting. Absolutely

enchanting. A dream. I think that is the word. (*Gallantly*) And doubly enchanting to come hither under the care of a guide so exceptional ... so ... youngly exquisite, may I say?

ALBERTO: No.

FRANCESCA: Thank you, Doctor.

ALBERTO: (*taking a bag from his shoulders*) I should think Aunt Cleofe must have stuffed a dozen electric irons in this damned bag.

He throws it to the ground. There is a muffled smash.

FRANCESCA: May I ask what you think you're doing? (*She goes over, picks up the bag, and looks inside.*)

ALBERTO: (*carelessly*) Something must have happened to something.

FRANCESCA: The rum has gone all over the cold omelette. Oh, how awful!

She throws the bag down, so that it drops on ALBERTO'S *foot.*

ALBERTO: (*jumping*) Well, don't dump the bag down on my foot! You seem to be in a very pleasant mood today, I must say.

FRANCESCA: Doctor, have you seen the spring?

THE DOCTOR: Yes. Charming, quite charming. Such lovely green grass; such velvety moss.

FRANCESCA: (*pointing*) And the ravine?

ALBERTO: Ravine, my foot! Why, if I went and stood up in it my head would poke over the top.

FRANCESCA: (*ostentatiously talking only to the* DOCTOR, *and pointing to where the rest of the party has gone*) I think this is far nicer than the other place, don't you, Doctor? You get a much finer view from here.

THE DOCTOR: Beautiful, beautiful! Picturesque. Yes. And what is *that*?

ALBERTO: (*crossly*) That, Doctor, is a mountain. What do you think it is? It's a mountain.

THE DOCTOR: What a sweeping immensity! So elevating to the thoughts. And the air so healthy, so balsamic. (*Explanatorily*) Owing to the presence of resin.

ALBERTO: In any case, I found this place before anyone else did: years ago; I was thirteen, or fourteen, at the most.

FRANCESCA: (*coldly*) You're wrong, Alberto dear. It was I who discovered it first.

ALBERTO: What? Nonsense! Who explored the palace first, me or you?

THE DOCTOR: The palace?

FRANCESCA: (*pointing to the ruined hut*) We call that the mountain-king's palace.

THE DOCTOR: Ah, yes, of course. I understand. The dear games of childhood. How sweet it is to recall them, is it not? And who was the *king* of the castle?

FRANCESCA: I was.

ALBERTO: No, you weren't. *I* was.

FRANCESCA: I'm sorry to contradict you, Alberto. *I* was.

ALBERTO: I'd like to know how a woman could be king of the castle? I merely ask.

FRANCESCA: Well, I was: that's all.

THE DOCTOR: Perhaps you were *both* king of the castle?

ALBERTO: (*indignantly*) No! *I* was! Whenever we came up to picnic at the Madonna, Francesca and I always brought our basket up here. I was king of the castle. You might just cast your mind back and recall whether or not you were my favourite slave? Were you, or weren't you?

FRANCESCA: (*aloofly*) Just as you wish. I should hate to upset you. (*She goes over to fill a glass of water at the spring.*)

THE DOCTOR: (*examining the hut, funereally*) I suppose this thing isn't dangerous? It seems firm enough. But those cracks provoke a little misgiving, rather.

FRANCESCA: Do taste the water, Doctor.

THE DOCTOR: Thank you. (*He does so, and splutters.*) Poooff!

ALBERTO: Nice taste, Doctor? Like bad eggs rather, isn't it?

THE DOCTOR: (*severely*) On the contrary, it's very good for the system. (*He sips, more gingerly.*) Sulphur. (*Sips again.*) Iron. (*Sips.*) And slight traces of arsenic. Very life-enhancing. Ah, what a pity-pity-pity we have no initiative in this country. If only this were America!

FRANCESCA: Don't you think this would be a wonderful place for us to have lunch?

THE DOCTOR: Are we going to eat *here*?

FRANCESCA: Yes. There's no one to bother us here.

THE DOCTOR: I . . . think it is a little bit cut off, isn't it? Isolated rather? And even a wee bit damp, I fear me.

FRANCESCA: Oh, Doctor, don't tell me you're afraid of the damp!

THE DOCTOR: Oh, no-no, I never said that, I never said I was. No-no. (*Pointing off-stage*) It's only that over there with the others, it's under cover. Sheltered, as it were. I observe a few little clouds gathering, a few little clouds in the sky. I would not like us to be the victims of one of the frequent mountain deluges.

ALBERTO: (*mischievously*) Doctor, I suppose you wouldn't like to call a deluge down upon us, by your magic arts?

THE DOCTOR: (*offended*) I am not aware that I command such arts, my friend.

FRANCESCA: (*hastily*) Good, then that's settled. We'll eat here. (*Casually*) And now someone will have to take the others their part of the cold omelette.

ALBERTO: (*suspiciously*) What was that?

FRANCESCA: Their part of it. The whole of the cold omelette is in here in the bag. You wouldn't like them all to die of hunger over there, would you? Without any cold omelette?

ALBERTO: (*sitting down, resolutely*) So, that's it! No, I won't. No, no, *no*. I'm not moving from here. Don't think it. One, I'm tired; two, it's too far; three, I don't want a piece taken out of my leg by one of those dogs; four, I'm not moving; five, I ...

FRANCESCA: (*icily*) No one ever expected so unselfish and kindly an action from *you*, Alberto. Why should they? I'm so sorry, Doctor, I'm sure *you* won't mind.

THE DOCTOR: (*sadly*) I ... I have to go all the way up there? To take the cold omelette?

FRANCESCA: I'm so sorry. It isn't very far.

THE DOCTOR: (*stoically*) I am ready. It is a pleasure for me to execute your commands. I *fly*. Oh. Look. Look. Have you noticed?

ALBERTO: What?

THE DOCTOR: The wind has changed. It has veered round, right round. Dear me. We can no longer exclude the possibility of a storm, I fear. No matter. I fly. I ... I suppose those dogs are quite safe?

ALBERTO: Just look them straight in the eye.

The DOCTOR, *with a cold glance at* ALBERTO, *withdraws. There is a renewed barking of dogs as he goes away. Cow-bells are also heard.*

THE DOCTOR: (*off—with nervous playfulness*) Down, down, there. Good dog, good doggy-woggy . . . (*His voice dies away.*)

FRANCESCA: (*calls after him*) Thank you, Doctor.

ALBERTO: Francesca. (*No reply.*) Francesca, what's the matter with you today?

FRANCESCA: (*contemptuously*) Nothing. It's you who seem upset, not me.

ALBERTO: Can't you understand that that was all nonsense down there? A mistake, that was all. That chap, Guido Consalvo . . . (*breaking off*) You know, you were quite right to send the silly devil to the station. It was a brainwave. (*He laughs.*) When I think of the old boy waiting for me there on the platform, all hot and sticky . . . and the train going in a few minutes. You know, Francesca, these business men never have a minute to spare. I bet he's got a ticket to America in his pocket for tomorrow. If he doesn't get to the boat in time tomorrow, the ticket will expire. And off he goes, on the ocean wave, forgetting and forgiving . . . Well, I hope he has a pleasant journey.

FRANCESCA: (*bitingly*) And the lady?

ALBERTO: Oh, she'll go with him. You don't want her to settle here for good, do you?

FRANCESCA: Do you know why I helped you? Because I felt sorry for you. You looked so frightened.

ALBERTO: Who? Me? Frightened? I was just holding

myself back, that was all. Why, I could have pulverised him there and then—like a fly. I'd just like to meet him again. I'd show him.

FRANCESCA: And I wasn't just sorry, Alberto. I was also pretty disgusted. Do you understand?

ALBERTO: But can't you see that you're wrong about all this? It's all perfectly innocent; it'd win a world championship for innocence. That lady is a widow; one of those extremely correct, irreproachable women. He's her brother, just her brother, that's all. Heaven knows what you've been imagining. There's been a silly little bit of gossip about absolutely nothing, and he's worried about it, that's all. Poor chap. It's all terribly simple and innocent. And tomorrow *he'll* be leaving, and *she'll* be leaving . . .

FRANCESCA: Are you quite certain of that?

ALBERTO: Did I tell you, or didn't I? They'll be on board ship, and everything will be dead and buried and forgotten? And you turn nasty over a trivial little thing like that. You enjoy ruining my last few hours here; the last moments I shall ever spend here. Ah, there used to be a time when we agreed about everything . . . You stuck up for me, and I stuck up for you . . .

FRANCESCA: (*mollified*) But, Alberto dear, that was what I was upset about. Surely you realise that? You used to be so frank with me the whole time. You told me everything. Everything. It was always just the two of us against everyone else, whatever happened. Do you really think those two are going away?

ALBERTO: (*looking at his watch*) They've already gone, my dear girl.

A very distant train whistle is heard from down in the valley.

The Train: Peeeeeeeee . . .

Alberto: Did you hear? The train—peeeeee . . . And tomorrow I shall be on it, too. Peeeeee . . . It means goodbye.

Francesca: Alberto.

Alberto: Yes?

Francesca: You'll . . . come back here sometimes?

Alberto: (*shrugging*) I don't know. Sometimes. Not very often, I'm afraid.

Francesca: Oooh! (*She clasps her ankle.*)

Alberto: What have you done?

Francesca. My ankle. Oooh.

Alberto: Hurt?

Francesca: Aaah! I can't put my foot down. Oh, Alberto, I think I've sprained it.

Alberto: (*indifferently*) Yes, it's an easy thing to do, up here.

Francesca: (*indignantly*) But, Alberto! Do at least please come and help me!

Alberto: (*shrugging*) I'm coming, I'm coming . . . What do you want me to do?

Francesca: You'll have to lift me up.

Alberto: Lift you up?

Francesca: Yes. And carry me. I can't put my foot to the ground. You know how it is with a sprain.

Alberto: Carry you? Where to?

Francesca: Why, up there. To Auntie.

Alberto: (*calmly*) Oh, no, I shan't. The ground's too uneven. And you're heavier than I am.

FRANCESCA: (*indignantly*) You . . . you refuse? You're going to leave me here?

ALBERTO: Of course, I'm not. I won't leave you. I'll stay with you. You could sit down for a bit, and wait. You'll be quite all right. The doctor will be back any minute. He's a big, hefty chap, and besides, he's used to these things. He's a doctor. He'll carry you. (*He helps her to sit down.*)

FRANCESCA: (*after a pause—shuddering*) So you . . . you'll make the doctor carry me?

ALBERTO: Yes. I was just saying: it's his job.

FRANCESCA: Ah, yes, it's his job. (*After a pause, calmly*) Alberto, look. I . . . I mustn't let the doctor carry me.

ALBERTO: What do you mean—mustn't?

FRANCESCA: (*enigmatically*) I mustn't, that's all.

ALBERTO: Why?

FRANCESCA: He would have to put his arms round me.

ALBERTO: Poor him. Well, he's not so ugly as all that.

FRANCESCA: On the contrary, I think he's very handsome.

ALBERTO: Well, there's no need to exaggerate.

FRANCESCA: I think he's a fine figure of a man. (*Modestly*) That's the reason, of course.

ALBERTO: What do you mean—that's the reason?

FRANCESCA: Well, of course. Surely you knew? With things as they are . . . it really wouldn't be quite nice for him to put his arms round me, just yet.

ALBERTO: (*after a silence*) You mean . . . you and the doctor . . . ?

FRANCESCA: I thought you'd probably noticed.

ALBERTO: (*surprised and indignant*) You and the doctor . . . there's a . . . *something* . . . between *you and him*?

FRANCESCA: I don't see what there is to be so surprised about.

ALBERTO: (*greatly annoyed*) So that was what your aunt was going on about. I see. Since when?

FRANCESCA: Oh, well . . . it's all rather vague, of course . . . at the moment. Very little has been actually said yet.

ALBERTO: And you really mean to say you . . . *like* that . . . that extraordinary *thing*?

FRANCESCA: I certainly don't dislike him. He's . . . I find him very interesting. I'm not saying he . . . exactly *thrills* me. Of course, but . . . he's a fine figure of a man. And there's his voice. It's so manly. Aunt Cleofe agrees with me.

ALBERTO: (*exploding*) Manly! Manly! The doctor's voice, manly! Why, he talks like this . . . baa-baa-baa! Like an old sheep . . . playing a trombone. (*He laughs satirically.*) The doctor—handsome! Why, he's like a . . . I don't know, an old monkey-nut. He's like an old umbrella-stand. He's disgusting. The thrilling doctor! Good heavens.

FRANCESCA: (*already sorry*) But I didn't say he thrilled me. You misunderstood me.

ALBERTO: That was what you said. I've never heard anything like it. It makes me feel quite sick. Here, in my tummy. (*Furiously*) And to think that I've always thought you were a person . . . above such things. Why, I'm ashamed even to think that you . . . oh!

FRANCESCA: (*in a low voice*) I'm a woman, you know, just like any other woman, Alberto.

ALBERTO: And I'm a fool! Why? Because I liked to think there was at least one girl in the world who was different from all the rest! I see now. I understand. Hence all those little tricks to try and get him up here alone, and send me away!

FRANCESCA: (*disheartened*) You know, Alberto, it's just possible you haven't understood *anything at all.*

ALBERTO: I see. I don't understand now, don't I? Very well, I'll go and shout for him. The thrilling doctor. Then he can look after your sprained ankle.

The dogs are heard barking again.

FRANCESCA: No, listen, Alberto.

ALBERTO: (*walking towards the path they have come up by*) He can carry you up there with his big manly arms around you.

FRANCESCA: (*pleading*) No, Alberto, don't. I haven't explained . . . (*Pause.*) What's the matter?

ALBERTO: (*whispers*) Damn it! Damn it! This is persecution. Consalvo is coming up here.

FRANCESCA: (*forgetting her ankle, runs across to see*) And Noemi, too. They're together this time. But you said they'd got to catch a boat for America.

ALBERTO: I only meant I was hoping they'd got to. What are we to do? (*Pleading*) Francesca, could you possibly . . .

FRANCESCA: (*maternal and decided*) Yes, Alberto, of course, I could. Leave them to me. I'll look after this.

ALBERTO: (*whispers*) Send them away. Send them away.

NOEMI *enters hurriedly, and rushes across to* ALBERTO.

NOEMI: Alberto! Consalvo's here: you *must* see him, and——

She breaks off. ALBERTO *has retreated into the hut. He can still be seen by the audience. The barking grows louder.* CONSALVO *is heard protesting.*

CONSALVO: (*off*) Why can't you keep those dogs off?

A VOICE: (*off*) They bain't doën nothen. Doän't ee go for to tease 'em.

CONSALVO: (*off*) Tease them! Good God in Heaven. (*Entering, exhausted and angry*) What sort of person do they think I am! Tease them, indeed!

FRANCESCA: (*sweetly*) Ah, good afternoon! We meet again.

CONSALVO: (*darkly*) Oh. It's you.

FRANCESCA: How are you?

CONSALVO: (*breathing heavily*) Dreadful. This heat's absolutely stifling. And the flies won't let me alone. Young lady, it appears it was quite untrue that there was anyone waiting at the station for me.

FRANCESCA: (*innocently*) I think you said it was Mr. Moesse you were expecting to meet you?

CONSALVO: I don't know who else you thought I was talking about.

FRANCESCA: But I thought you'd let him know you were coming?

CONSALVO: (*angrily*) Well, so I had!

FRANCESCA: But where else can he have expected to meet you except at the station? That's what I told you.

CONSALVO: He thought it was safer to run away. Well, he was mistaken, that's all.

NOEMI: But, Consalvo, do please listen to me!

CONSALVO: You keep out of this, Noemi. He's run

away to the Madonna of the Mountain. That's where he's gone.

NOEMI: But do at least try and keep *calm*. Try and get your breath back.

CONSALVO: I'll get that back after I've caught that man. And I shall catch him. I *intend* to catch him. (*He is about to sit down.*)

FRANCESCA: (*kindly*) Did I hear you say that Mr. Moesse had gone to the Madonna of the Mountain?

CONSALVO: (*sulkily*) Yes. To the Madonna of the Mountain.

FRANCESCA: And do *you* want to go to the Madonna of the Mountain?

CONSALVO: Yes.

FRANCESCA: Well, that's easy. (*Angelically*) The Madonna of the Mountain is . . . just up there. (*She points.*)

CONSALVO: (*horrified*) Up there!

FRANCESCA: Yes, can you see? Just up there, high up, that little white square thing.

CONSALVO: (*sadly*) I see it.

FRANCESCA: It's not so very far. Not so far as it looks. The important thing is not to hurry too fast. That's the secret, up in the mountains.

CONSALVO: So I've discovered.

NOEMI: But, Consalvo, do listen to me . . .

CONSALVO: (*retreating*) Come on, Noemi. I felt a spot of rain.

The dogs are heard again as he goes away.

CONSALVO: (*off*) You silly fool! Why can't you keep the dogs to yourself?

A VOICE: I tell ee, sir, doän't ee go for to tease 'em!

NOEMI *has followed him off, taking care to leave her raincoat behind. She at once reappears in order to retrieve it.*

NOEMI: (*in a low voice to* ALBERTO) Alberto. I really can't understand what you're up to, Alberto. I'm not letting you down, I'm helping you all I can. You know, I'm for you and against him, but I really can't see why you . . .

FRANCESCA: (*coming forward; hostile and sarcastic*) What is it you can't see?

NOEMI: (*casts a contemptuous glance at her, and addresses* ALBERTO.) I don't understand, Alberto, why you insist on provoking him like this. It makes him much worse. You don't know what Consalvo's like. Once he starts he goes on to the end. You know I'm on your side . . . but I do think you ought to face up to it and see him; and try and settle things. Especially as I'm here to support you.

FRANCESCA: So that's what you want, is it?

NOEMI: My dear, I really can't see why you have to keep interfering like this.

FRANCESCA: It's you who are interfering with us. We were perfectly happy till you came.

NOEMI: I don't know what business of yours this is.

FRANCESCA: And I don't know who asked you to come here.

ALBERTO: (*desperately, from the hut*) Girls, it's coming on to rain!

CONSALVO: (*from the distance*) Noemi!

NOEMI: (*calls*) I'm coming! (*To* FRANCESCA) I'm here to stand by Alberto's side, if you want to know.

FRANCESCA: Alberto has no need of anyone like you to stand by his side.

NOEMI: I suppose you think you are enough!

It begins to rain. Occasional thunder is heard.

FRANCESCA: Oh, *I'm* not in the habit of making long journeys in order to protect young men.

NOEMI: And I'm not in the habit of traipsing about over hills with them and sticking to them like glue.

FRANCESCA: And I don't deceive my relations by sending them on ahead, like some I could mention.

NOEMI: You silly little fool. You empty-headed little idiot. (*With meaning*) I pity *you*, my dear. Just wait till you're told.

ALBERTO: (*desperately*) Girls! You'll get soaked to the skin.

CONSALVO: (*off*) Noemi!

FRANCESCA: Alberto will tell me all about you.

NOEMI: (*contemptuous, precise and meaningful*) All? Will he? Good. And then perhaps you'll have the sense ... to understand *his* position; *my* position; and the position of *both* of us. Good afternoon.

She recedes on this farewell. The thunder dies away and the rain diminishes. The sky is already beginning to lighten.

ALBERTO: (*after a pause, timidly*) Francesca.

FRANCESCA: You fill me with disgust. Go away.

ALBERTO: I only want to explain ...

FRANCESCA: (*fiercely*) Leave me alone. Go away.

ALBERTO: ... to explain what happened, so that you shan't think ... Francesca, it's such a little thing, really it is. You've no idea what a tiny little thing it all is.

FRANCESCA: I wish to hear nothing about it.

ALBERTO: (*becoming more disturbed*) Do you know what it's all been caused by? All this trouble and fuss? People sending telegrams and bothering people like this? It's all been caused by a simple little outing in a rowing-boat; the sea was as smooth as glass. Everyone was rowing on it. In little boats. Is there any reason why I shouldn't have gone out in one like everyone else? That's all it was. A little outing in a rowing-boat. That's all.

FRANCESCA: I've told you I wish to know nothing about it.

ALBERTO: An outing in a rowing-boat. How was I to know that a great typhoon sort of thing was going to blow up before I knew where I was? It was terrible. Winds. Waves. Like the end of the world. Like a hurricane. Or a tempest. Why, the boat almost capsized! We might both have been drowned, just like that, swept away! You ought to be glad we escaped. We were like a couple of drowned mice. We might both have caught our deaths, quite easily.

FRANCESCA: Both of whom?

ALBERTO: Why, I . . . and that girl, Noemi. It wasn't my fault the wind carried us lower down, was it?

FRANCESCA: What do you mean—lower down?

ALBERTO: What do you think I mean? Lower down. Lower down on the beach. A bit of deserted sand; I don't know where it was; it was raining like a tap; thunder and lightning. A flood almost. (*As though he had now told all*) That was all. *That* is my terrible crime.

FRANCESCA: Is that all?

ALBERTO: Of course, it's all. I had to pay for the boat as well. (*Angrily*) Did they expect us to stay there on the beach, catching pneumonia? Or waiting to be struck by lightning? Fortunately, there was a large hut. We went inside to shelter.

FRANCESCA: Ah, yes. And then?

ALBERTO: Then nothing. It was a deposit place for cement and hydraulic lime. That's all. If the people it belonged to hadn't been such fools, nothing would have happened. How could anybody think we'd gone in there to steal cement and hydraulic lime? It's mad. I don't know who it was, but someone heard a noise, and thought that there were thieves in the hut.

FRANCESCA: (*angrily*) And then?

ALBERTO: Why, they called the police, of course. Can you imagine anything so silly? I can't tell you the stupid things they said, all the lies they made up. Why, we still had them *on*!

FRANCESCA: Had what on?

ALBERTO: (*indignantly*) Our bathing-dresses! They said we'd taken them off to dry ourselves. It just wasn't true! We still had them on. Everything was perfectly in order. How could they expect us to be carrying identity cards and documents in our bathing-dresses? Have you cver heard anything so stupid?

FRANCESCA: Well?

ALBERTO: Nothing. The fool of a policeman telephoned all over the place, and crowds of people came rushing up. Fortunately, we were recognised at once and everything was perfectly all right. (*Virtuously*) Naturally, no one thought *I* was the sort of person that creeps round stealing cement and hydraulic lime. (*A pause.*)

FRANCESCA: (*coldly*) What *is* hydraulic lime?

Alberto: (*impatiently*) I don't know what it is. It's *lime*. Of some sort.

Francesca: (*distantly*) Well, you were very lucky.

Alberto: Yes, but do you know what happened? The policeman said I'd called him a fool and punched him. Can you imagine me doing such a thing, Francesca?

Francesca: No. What happened then?

Alberto: They arrested me.

Francesca: Well?

Alberto: They took us away. In our bathing-dresses. When you think about it, well, it would almost . . .

Francesca: (*cold and angry*) Make anyone laugh, wouldn't it? Is that what you mean?

Alberto: (*as though this were unimportant*) They say we shall have to appear in court.

Francesca: In court?

Alberto: Oh, it won't be anything important. It shouldn't last more than three years, they say. Though, of course, there'll be a pile of expenses to pay. No, that's not the trouble.

Francesca: Why, is there something more?

Alberto: (*as though recounting a complicated but rather amusing and interesting story*) You see, it's Noemi's relations really. They have terribly old-fashioned ideas. They've gone absolutely wild over this. Well, you saw. The extraordinary thing is they're not *her* relations at all, really, they're her husband's relations. She's a widow. He's dead. The whole thing's mad, of course. And these relations—are you listening to me?

Francesca: I'm listening.

Alberto: Well, actually they're also the shareholders in Consalvo's bank. He's a banker, you see.

And also he's Noemi's brother. And he's the man who's giving me this job in the bank. He's the manager of it.

FRANCESCA: (*her head is beginning to go round*) The manager!

ALBERTO: Yes, because, you see, Noemi very kindly got her brother to give me this job in his bank. It was she who did that. I was to have started there the day after tomorrow. Or some time. But, you see, *now*, Consalvo has gone crazy, too. Because what's happened is that Noemi's late husband's relations—the people I think I told you about, who are so old-fashioned—*they* say that if he doesn't get things cleared up they'll withdraw their capital. Do you follow me? They'll withdraw their capital.

FRANCESCA: Why?

ALBERTO: Because of the newspapers.

FRANCESCA: Newspapers?

ALBERTO: Yes, of course, didn't I tell you? Down there on the beach in the hut some newspapermen came, you see; and so a rumour has got about—a rumour that they, the relations of Noemi's late husband, will withdraw their capital; and so the customers of the bank have started to talk and spread rumours, and there's a panic started, and if Consalvo can't get things put straight, they're already saying there'll be a failure.

FRANCESCA: A failure?

ALBERTO: But what on earth should I know about all this? I can't tell you what a mess everything has got into. Noemi is on my side, because she's above all these things, of course; she's a sensible modern woman. Can you imagine what I felt when they took our photograph and published it?

FRANCESCA: A photograph!

ALBERTO: Yes, in the newspapers.

FRANCESCA: In bathing-dresses?

ALBERTO: Yes. But, of course, it's all very indistinct in the picture, no one could possibly tell it was us . . . If it weren't for . . .

FRANCESCA: Weren't for what?

ALBERTO: Well, how was I to know? I gave them our names and addresses. They printed them, under the photo.

FRANCESCA: I think I'm beginning to understand. What happened after that?

ALBERTO: Well, what do you think? Gossip, scandals . . . cartoons in the papers . . . and a comic song. They're singing it in one of the revues. (*With sudden anger*) Well, is it fair, do you think? Is it right that Consalvo should chase after me like this and cause all this trouble? Just for a row in a boat. (*A long silence.*) Francesca . . . (*Silence. She has her back to him.*) Francesca say it if you think it. Am I . . . Do *you* think I'm a criminal, too?

FRANCESCA: (*bending over the provisions*) No, Alberto, you're exactly what you've always been: ever since you were a little boy. And I have always liked you just as you are. Come and eat.

ALBERTO: Eat? But they'll be coming back.

FRANCESCA: Of course. But let's eat. And while we're eating, we can think . . . what we shall have to do. Because it's quite clear I shall have to help you in this, too, Alberto. It's I who'll have to get you out of trouble again. What's the matter? What are you staring at?

ALBERTO: You, Francesca. How very good you are . . . yes, certainly, let's eat . . . and think. Look: we'll put my jacket on the ground, shall we? The grass is wet.

FRANCESCA: (*affectionately*) Give it to me. You don't know how to do anything. Aren't you cold?

ALBERTO: (*adapting himself with great readiness to the rôle of spoilt child*) No, no.

FRANCESCA: (*brusquely, handing him the flask of rum, and a glass*) Drink a drop of this.

ALBERTO: (*as he drinks*) You know, Francesca, there are some things you can't understand. You're the serious type. In some things you don't even seem like a girl at all.

FRANCESCA: (*with lowered gaze*) Don't you think so?

ALBERTO: No. You might be a boy. Now, that woman Noemi's quite diff——

FRANCESCA: (*interrupting affectionately*) Don't tell me anything, Alberto. I already know everything. And we have so little time. Consalvo will be back here any minute. And in that little time we have to think of something that will settle things once and for all. Haven't we?

ALBERTO: (*happy that someone is looking after him*) Certainly. Sure.

FRANCESCA: (*pointing to the tart; maternally*) More tart?

ALBERTO: (*graciously*) Just one slice.

FRANCESCA: No, I'll cut it for you. (*Joking, but agitated also*) Aren't I your slave? Your favourite slave . . . ?

ALBERTO: (*in difficulties with the tart*) The crust keeps breaking . . .

FRANCESCA: (*cautiously*) Alberto, have you any idea what those people really want of you?

ALBERTO: (*mouth full*) Me?

FRANCESCA: What Noemi meant, for example, when she said you must make up your mind and face up to it.

ALBERTO: Face up to what Consalvo had to say, she meant.

FRANCESCA: And what is Consalvo after?

ALBERTO: Consalvo? Well, *I* think he's out of his mind.

FRANCESCA: No, perhaps not quite out of it. (*Offering the flask*) A little more rum? Alberto ... I'd do anything in the world to get you out of this mess. Do you realise that? And perhaps there is one way. Even if it meant I had to ... *sacrifice* myself ... I'd do it willingly. Do you remember once? I even lent you some money ... which you never paid me back? I'm ... very fond of you, Alberto. More than you think. I know that sometimes I'm rude to you; short with you perhaps.

ALBERTO: (*mouth full*) It's character, Francesca. It's all a question of character. You know my Aunt Fausta? She's just the same. She's always been absolutely unbearable ever since I can remember. Character, that's what it is.

FRANCESCA: (*distressed, earnestly*) But I'm not like that at all, Alberto! My character ... is gentle, and submissive, and affectionate.

ALBERTO: Oh, I know. But every so often—bang! And something awful pops out.

FRANCESCA: Oh, Alberto, you mustn't think that! I

can't bear it! I'm a good girl, Alberto. I'm cheerful. I'm very fond of . . . everyone.

ALBERTO: (*conceding the point*) Well, who said you weren't? You *are* a good girl.

FRANCESCA: (*embarrassed*) I know I'm not a rich girl. That's true; but even that's a good thing sometimes.

ALBERTO: Oh, yes, quite. It moulds people; shapes them.

FRANCESCA: Of course, it does. It's meant I've learnt to do things in the house; I'm very good at some of them. You see this jacket? I made it myself. I can't tell you what a bother it was to get right. But I wouldn't change it for that dress Noemi was wearing. It's come out rather well, don't you think?

ALBERTO: (*feeling it*) Yes, it looks very well on you. (*He has marked it with jam.*) Damn. Sorry. My fingers were sticky from the tart: I've smudged it. (*He attempts to clean it by rubbing it with his elbow.*)

FRANCESCA: It doesn't matter, Alberto, don't bother. You'll only make it worse. I'll wash it off at the spring.

ALBERTO: I trail disaster with me wherever I go . . .

FRANCESCA: But, Alberto, that's what I like about you. Didn't you know? It's rather as though you'd stayed a boy, and only I had grown up. And you ought to realise that. (*Tremulously*) I've never played with any other boy except you, Alberto. Always with you. With you. (*Her voice is shaking, and she doesn't know how to begin.*) How . . . fresh the air is, isn't it? And how lovely and clear the sky is now.

ALBERTO: (*lazily, without turning round*) Yes. Lot of country you can see from here, can t you? What a view!

FRANCESCA: Alberto, listen. There's something I wanted to say to you. I wanted to say . . . give me the flask, will you? (*She takes it, and a glass, and drinks rather liberally; then she laughs.*) Ah, that's better. It gives you courage, I always think. Strength. (*Determinedly*) Listen, Alberto, you're really a boy, do you see? You're not a bad boy . . . but you don't think, you say silly things, you tell little fibs. It's because of that that some people think something may happen to you.

ALBERTO: (*rather struck*) What sort of something?

FRANCESCA: I don't know . . . accidents, designing people. If there's no one to look after you, who can tell what troubles and disgraces you may get yourself into? Poor Alberto.

ALBERTO: Damn it, Francesca, what an extraordinary way to talk to anyone.

FRANCESCA: One can put up with other people being unhappy. It's almost natural. But not you. It's so nice to see you happy. To see you suffer must be . . . I don't know, heartbreaking.

ALBERTO: (*simply*) Oh, naturally.

FRANCESCA: You see, you're so simple and trusting, Alberto. For example, whenever there's any false money in the village, who is it always palmed off on? You.

ALBERTO: Oh, but I always manage to pass it on to someone else. I'm very good at it.

FRANCESCA: There ought to be someone near you . . . to protect you.

ALBERTO: What do you mean—protect me?

FRANCESCA: It's just that . . . you'd be better off if there were. And there's your health too. You're not at all strong, you know.

ALBERTO: Not strong!

FRANCESCA: No. Anyone can see you lead quite the wrong sort of life. What you need is someone by you to keep you well, and happy, and clean.

ALBERTO: (*much offended*) Oh, so I'm not clean now!

FRANCESCA: No, please try and understand me, Alberto.

ALBERTO: I'm *terribly* clean!

FRANCESCA: (*rather huskily*) Alberto, why don't you get married? (*Brief pause.*) After all, there comes a time when ... naturally, one has to choose very carefully ... among the people who are near to one. I know that there ... *is* someone, certainly ... who ... in whom you could have complete confidence, and who has shown in the past how very reliable she can be ... and how fond of you she really is.

ALBERTO: (*laboriously hunting for a cigarette*) I ... I'm not the boasting sort—but as a matter of fact, I get on pretty well with *most* women.

FRANCESCA: I think it must be ... so beautiful to live with someone forever. To stay and listen to them the whole time. To watch them eat their dinner and drink their coffee afterwards. And to tell them everything that's happened during the day ... such lovely evenings together. One would be ... so very *happy*.

ALBERTO: (*during an acrobatic experiment in lighting a match*) Oh, I've thought of that, of course, too. People are bound to get married eventually, it's only natural.

FRANCESCA: (*huskily*) Alberto. It's quite obvious what that girl Noemi is after. And Consalvo. "Make up your mind," she said. "Get things straight" ... etcetera. Don't you see ?

ALBERTO: (*finally lighting the match*) What? Do you mean . . . ?

FRANCESCA: However you look at it, there's only one way of getting things straight, so far as they're concerned.

ALBERTO: Oh, I don't really think so, you know.

FRANCESCA: Oh, yes, my dear.

ALBERTO: No, but think . . . you may be right about Consalvo; but what about Noemi? . . . Good heavens, she laughs at all that sort of thing. She's sophisticated.

FRANCESCA: How simple you are, Alberto. She's a woman.

ALBERTO: But she's on my side. She's my ally.

FRANCESCA: But do you think she hasn't any secret thoughts of her own about you, deep down? If she hadn't she wouldn't have come rushing up here like this. I may be a country girl, but I have my eyes about me. Listen to me, Alberto. They'll both be back in a few moments. It's quite clear what they're after. If they don't find you here, what will they do? Run after you.

ALBERTO: (*cheerfully*) Well, I'll run faster, that's all.

FRANCESCA: No, no, no, that's not the way. (*Embarrassment creeps into her voice.*) I'm quite sure that what you ought to do is to wait for them quite quietly, here; and tell them . . . something definite . . . which will settle things once and for all . . . both for them and for us. (*Stammering*) Before *they* begin talking about marriage, don't you see, you ought to throw it in their teeth from the start. I am here . . . if you like I'll do it for you, gladly . . . You must shut them up at once; make them look silly. Like someone running to catch a train and finding it's already gone. Tell them it's useless to make so much fuss. Because you've already ... made up your mind. (*A pause.*)

ALBERTO: (*getting up, thoughtfully*) You know ... that *is* an idea.

FRANCESCA: (*moved and ashamed*) Oh, Alberto, you must understand me. I'm not very good at explaining.

ALBERTO: (*absently*) Oh, no, you're very good at it. Very.

FRANCESCA: You can imagine how awkward it is for a young woman ... to be the one to speak first ... in things like this.

ALBERTO: (*who has been following his own train of thought*) Yes, I see it all now. All the little manœuvres, the little subterfuges ...

FRANCESCA: (*overcome with shame*) Oh, Alberto ... no, no, no. Those weren't subterfuges. It's just that ... when a woman feels fond of someone ... she naturally thinks of marriage. Women think of these things from girlhood onwards ... having a home and ba ... the cradle. It's what we're made for; and sometimes it may be necessary to make things up, so that the man shall understand. It's a thing we have to be forgiven for. It's because women grow fond, Alberto. They ... they fall in love.

The sound of a bell and then a distant hymn are heard from the Madonna of the Mountain.

FRANCESCA: (*deeply moved*) It's the benediction, Alberto. Let's kneel down.

ALBERTO: We shall get our clothes dirty.

FRANCESCA: It doesn't matter. Come and kneel close

to me. The Madonna of the Mountain has granted so many people's prayers.

ALBERTO: M'm? Oh . . . all right.

They kneel, and remain thus until the hymn comes to an end. FRANCESCA *makes the sign of the cross.*

FRANCESCA: Amen.

ALBERTO: (*absently*) What? Oh, yes. Amen. (*Rising decisively*) Francesca, you were quite right to speak to me like that. You've literally opened my eyes for me.

FRANCESCA: (*pale*) Really and truly, Alberto?

ALBERTO: You've made up my mind for me. It shall be exactly as you say.

FRANCESCA: (*almost speechless*) Oh, Alberto . . .

ALBERTO: Yes, you've decided for me. How odd I never thought of it myself. It's the one solution that . . . solves everything. I shall tell Consalvo the minute he comes back. It's no use beating about the bush, is it?

FRANCESCA: (*transfigured*) Oh, Alberto.

ALBERTO: After all, men are made for settling down. Especially when circumstances like this . . . well, almost . . . insist on it. You know what I mean.

FRANCESCA: Oh, God, how beautiful everything is . . . I could almost die of happiness.

ALBERTO: After all, people can't stay in a shell forever, can they? You have to think. Work things out. Think of your position, your whole life, your career.

FRANCESCO: Yes, Alberto.

ALBERTO: Yes. And after all, why should I shut my eyes to the fact that the girl's brother is an important bank manager?

FRANCESCA: Wh—wh—whose brother?

ALBERTO: Why, hers—Noemi's. He'll make a splendid career for me. I'll tell him the minute he comes. I'll say to him: "Dear brother-in-law, spare your breath, I thought of it even before you did; you can order the wedding cake at once." That's what I'll say. And so: honour will be restored. The relations pacified. The dead at peace. Consalvo jubilant. And Noemi—poor girl, what pathetic little shifts and dodges she's had to get up to—telegrams, and clambering all the way up here like this. It really has got a grip on her, hasn't it? Poor little widow . . . where are you going, Francesca?

FRANCESCA: (*hardly knowing what she is doing or saying, has moved away from him with a few uncertain steps, to hide her face from him.*) I . . . I'm going to . . . I . . . I want . . . to wash my jacket.

ALBERTO: How sensible you are, Francesca. I might never have thought of it myself. It was very clever of you. It's just like mathematics really—the position, the bank, the relations, the rowing-boat, Consalvo getting so angry—it all fits in, doesn't it, just like a jig-saw puzzle? I'm not all that enthusiastic about Noemi, of course, but when all's said and done, she *is* a lady, she wears awfully nice clothes . . . and she must be quite well off, too. Yes, my dear, Francesca, we all have to pause and think sometimes; and marriages of convenience—they're called that, you know—have always been the best. Youth doesn't last forever. What's the matter? You crying? Because of the jacket?

FRANCESCA: (*trying to restrain her tears*) I was thinking . . . everything has been so beautiful . . . I keep thinking of how happy we've been . . .

ALBERTO: (*affectionately putting an arm round her*

shoulders and shaking her) You're feeling all right, aren't you? You haven't had too much of that rum?

FRANCESCA: No, no.

ALBERTO: (*leading her to the edge of the 'ravine'; the sun has begun to set.*) Look. What a wonderful sky it is, isn't it? You know, Francesca, life isn't such a bad thing after all. What colours! (*Calls suddenly*) Noemi-i-i-! Noemi-i-i-i! There they are. Give me that. (*He snatches* FRANCESCA'S *coloured handkerchief from her shoulders and waves with it, calling*) Ye-es! We're he-ere! Come ba-ack! (*To* FRANCESCA) I'll speak at once, and get it over. It's much the best thing. (*Calling again*) Come he-ere! Yes, they're coming. Good. Oh, Francesca, we shall have such a lovely house . . . and who'll come and see us every now and then? Our dear little Francesca, Aunt Cleofe the second, eh? (*Calls*) Oohoo! Oohoo! (*To* FRANCESCA) Oh, Francesca, you don't know how fond I am of you, old boy. We'll invite you to come and stay with us whenever you like. And to the wedding, of course. Because actually all this is really due to you, you know. (*Calls*) Oohoo! Oohoo! Oohoo! . . .

FRANCESCA, *in the extremity of despair, seems undecided whether to burst into sobs or to throw herself into the 'ravine'; instead she suddenly pushes* ALBERTO *over the edge with both her hands. He disappears at once.* FRANCESCA *is immediately filled with wild distress and falls on her knees, bending over the edge.*

FRANCESCA: (*in terror*) Oh, my God! (*To herself*) What have I done? I didn't mean to! Oh, God! (*Calling*) Alberto! Alberto! Are you all right? (*To the mountain*) Help! Help! Come quickly! (*Leaning over the edge*)

Alberto, my own Alberto! Please! Alberto! Please try and climb up. Do try!

ALBERTO: (*in a distant muffled voice—the words are not heard*) I might have been killed.

FRANCESCA: (*calling*) Help! Doctor! Help! Yes, come up here! Gently, Alberto: steady! Here! Hold on here! Give me your hand.

ALBERTO's *head appears over the edge.*

FRANCESCA: Hold me tightly. Up ... up ... Oh, Alberto! Oh, my dear. Please. Please speak to me. Answer me.

She helps him up. His face and hands are covered with scratches, his mouth full of dirt.

ALBERTO: (*spluttering*) You are a stupid clumsy girl, Francesca. You brushed up against me. You're always the same. You never notice what you're doing or where you're going. I might have hurt myself. (*He is clearly unaware that she has actually pushed him over.*)

FRANCESCA: (*faintly*) Oh, Alberto, what a terrible thing. Have you broken anything? How do you feel?

ALBERTO: It was full of nettles.

FRANCESCA: Don't talk. Lie down here. Here. Keep still; and quiet.

ALBERTO: (*beginning to feel frightened*) M-m-must I lie down?

FRANCESCA: Yes, it'll be safer. Tell me: can you feel anything?

ALBERTO: No. Nothing. (*Winces.*) Ooh.

FRANCESCA: Oh, dear ... (*Calls*) Doctor! Help! Quick! Help! Doctor!

ALBERTO: Fran . . . cesca, don't do that. You frighten me as well.

FRANCESCA: Keep calm. Darling, try . . . try and move your toes, if you can . . . Can you?

ALBERTO: Yes . . . I can.

FRANCESCA: Thank God. It means your dorsal column is intact.

ALBERTO: (*terrified*) What? Good heavens! Ooooh!

FRANCESCA: (*calls*) Help! . . . Wait: there's the doctor's bag, I'll bandage you . . .

ALBERTO: (*nervously*) Bandage *what*?

FRANCESCA: I don't know. Your face. There's blood on it.

ALBERTO: Blood!

FRANCESCA: Keep still.

ALBERTO: Oh God, what's going to happen to me? What's going to happen to me?

FRANCESCA: (*energetically slapping plasters on to his face*) Do you feel better like that? M'm?

ALBERTO: (*unable to speak because of a plaster across his mouth*) I . . . don't know . . . what will become of me . . .

The DOCTOR *enters.*

THE DOCTOR: (*panting*) Calm, calm, calm. Keep quite calm.

FRANCESCA: Oh, Doctor, thank God, you've come.

THE DOCTOR: Keep calm. (*Feeling* ALBERTO's *pulse*) Courage, Alberto! We're here. Look up! Open the eyes. Look up. Quietly.

Night is beginning to fall.

FRANCESCA: Please, Doctor, do do something.

THE DOCTOR: Quiet-ly. Don't be afraid, my dear,

have no fear. I've seen far worse than this in my time. I've seen men smashed up completely. Like pulp. Some of the cases I've been called into have been all to pieces; literally in pieces. Do you know I once saw a man with only half a . . .

FRANCESCA: Oh, Doctor, no, don't!

THE DOCTOR: I thought nothing of it. Where's my bag? Can he speak?

FRANCESCA: He could till a few moments ago.

THE DOCTOR: Well, why can't he now?

ALBERTO: (*spluttering*) The p . . . laster . . .

THE DOCTOR: (*shouts to* ALBERTO) Alberto! Can you hear me? Eh? Can you speak? What happened? Did you fall? Over the cliff?

ALBERTO: . . .

THE DOCTOR: He says yes. Good. Excellent. Excellent. Now: let's see.

OFELIA: (*loudly as she bursts in*) Alberto! My Alberto! Oh, the poor lamb. Can you hear me, Alberto? It's me: your Aunt Ofelia! Say you can hear me! (*Much louder*) Tell me you can hear me!

ALBERTO: (*annoyed, lifting up one of the plasters*) Of course I can hear you! Don't make all that noise.

THE DOCTOR: Quiet-ly. Breathe in. Breathe out.

OFELIA: Doctor, Doctor: tell me how he is.

THE DOCTOR: (*after a series of professional examination grunts, during which the others listen in religious silence, rises and says with disgust*) Why, he's as well as I am!

ALBERTO: (*rising: anxiously*) I shan't suffer from delayed cerebral shock, shall I?

OFELIA: Or internal concussion, will he, Doctor? That's worse, far worse.

CLEOFE: (*entering*) What a lot of nonsense. I told you there was nothing the matter.

OFELIA: (*with enigmatic calm*) Oh, no. Nothing. Nothing. Just a little fall over a cliff.

CLEOFE: Cliff! It's just a ditchful of nettles!

OFELIA: It was a cliff! Suppose he'd bounced!

CLEOFE: Well, he isn't a rubber ball, is he?

OFELIA: We should have a corpse at our feet.

CLEOFE: He oughtn't to drink so much rum.

OFELIA: There was no question of rum. (*Her voice becomes solemn.*) Luckily, I was there. With *these*. Alberto's late uncle's marine binoculars.

A silence falls. They all turn to FRANCESCA, *who stands there, absent and indifferent, apparently staring into the distance.*

OFELIA: Francesca: perhaps you can tell us how Alberto fell over that cliff?

FRANCESCA (*absently*) I pushed him over.

ALBERTO: *Eh?*

OFELIA: And why did you push him over?

FRANCESCA: (*absently*) I just wanted to push him over, that was all.

OFELIA: Dear Alberto, she wanted to kill you. I saw it all. With my own eyes. And these. (*She means the binoculars.*)

ALBERTO: She wanted to . . . ?

OFELIA: She wanted to kill you; yes!

ALBERTO: But why? Why?

NOEMI: (*suddenly entering; calmly and spitefully*) Why? Why, because she's in love with you, darling. She's wildly, madly in love with you.

ALBERTO: (*flabbergasted*) *Eh?*

NOEMI: She loves you. Hopelessly, of course. She loves you . . . and we all know what she is . . . a little girl from the country whom no one pays any attention to, and who doesn't know how to dress, and hasn't a penny in her pocket . . .

CLEOFE: (*indignantly*) She has an insurance policy which matures the minute she's sixty-five!

NOEMI: A little snake in the grass: and *very* hypocritical, and *very* calculating, and very, *very* jealous . . .

ALBERTO: (*suddenly wild with anger, tears off his last bandages.*) If you dare say another word against that girl, I'll slap your face. If you want to know . . .

CONSALVO: (*entering and extending a finger towards* ALBERTO) If *you* want to know, sir, people can't go on trying to take in other people forever. (*Solemnly*) Are you, or are you not, Mr. Alberto Moesse?

ALBERTO: (*beside himself with rage*) Yes, sir. I am. I am, and I warn you, for your own sake, to get from under my feet! Get out of my way! . . . Francesca! . . . (*Surprised*) Francesca, where are you? Francesca!

But FRANCESCA *has disappeared.*

THE OTHERS: Francesca!
Where has she gone? Francesca!
Francesca, where you are?

THE DOCTOR: (*politely*) I have the most melancholy forebodings, you know.

THE OTHERS: (*scattering as they begin to look for her*) Look for her! Call her! Francesca! Francesca! Oh, my God, how dark it's getting. Francesca! . . .

ALBERTO: (*with tears in his voice; to* NOEMI *and*

CONSALVO) If anything happens to that girl I'll kill you! I'll kill you both! (*He goes off, calling*) Francesca! Where are you? Answer me! Francescaaaaaaa!

The stage is almost completely dark as the CURTAIN FALLS.

ACT THREE

A room in the house of one of the local farms. There are a number of doors, one of which leads to the cow-shed; there is a lunette over this, with bars. Another door leads to the kitchen. A few hours have passed since the preceding act.

The room is empty; the fire is lit. A knocking is heard at an outer door. Pause.

ALBERTO'S VOICE (*as he knocks at the door again*) Ho, there! Is anyone in? Open the door, please, will you?

A young FARMER *enters from the kitchen and crosses the room, switching on a light as he goes out to open the outer door; he re-enters, preceded by* ALBERTO, *who is soaked to the skin.*

THE FARMER: (*laughs without apparent reason, then asks innocently*) Is it raining, sir?

ALBERTO: (*after a withering glance at the man*) Have you seen a girl? Francesca her name is. A dark girl, rather pretty, with a blue dress and a white jacket.

THE FARMER: (*thinks*) A . . . a girl, you said, sir?

ALBERTO: (*furiously*) Yes, a girl!

THE FARMER: Yes, I see, sir. What would she be doing?

ALBERTO: How should *I* know? She's been seen near here.

THE FARMER: Where was she going, sir?

ALBERTO: If I knew, I wouldn't be here asking you.

THE FARMER: In a blue dress, did you say, sir?

ALBERTO: And a white jacket.

THE FARMER: I'll go and ask the wife, sir. (*He crosses to the kitchen door.*) Would you be the girl's father, sir?

ALBERTO: (*outraged*) Father! I ... I'm a friend of hers!

THE FARMER: Ah, yes, I see, sir. A friend. I'll just ask the wife, sir. (*Goes out.*)

ALBERTO *looks round; and suddenly observes, hanging up before the fire to dry*, FRANCESCA'S *jacket. He seizes it and runs to the door where the* FARMER *has disappeared; stops and listens; then goes quickly back to the fire and replaces the jacket. He assumes a nonchalant air as the* FARMER *returns.*

THE FARMER: (*re-entering*) No, sir. She hasn't. My wife says she hasn't seen any girl around this way, sir.

ALBERTO: (*who has expected this*) Well, well, never mind. I didn't really expect she would have. (*Looking round*) And how has the hay done this year?

THE FARMER: (*looking at him distrustfully*) Well ... it might be worse, sir. It doesn't do to complain. My wife wondered if you'd looked over the Lame Goat, sir?—that cliff just the other side of the road. There's a sheer drop there, forty feet or more. You never know what's going to happen there, when the weather's like this. The path's very slippery, you see. Poor girl. Let's hope ... well ...

ALBERTO: Let's hope, yes. (*Anxious to linger, he points towards the door of the cow-shed.*) And the cows this year, the milk, and so on, how's all that done?

THE FARMER: Well ... it might be worse, sir: it ... it ...

ALBERTO: (*cheerfully*) Doesn't do to complain, does it?

The noise of a motor-horn is heard outside; then violent knocking at the door.

CONSALVO: (*outside*) Open the door, please! Do you mind opening the door?

ALBERTO: (*pointing to the kitchen door*) Could I slip out that way?

THE FARMER: Well, that just leads into the back-yard, sir . . .

ALBERTO: Good, thank you: good evening. (*He makes for the door.*)

THE FARMER: . . . Evening, sir . . . (*Goes off-stage to the outer door; and is heard saying*) Who is it?

CONSALVO: (*outside*) Friends, my good man, friends!

ALBERTO, *instead of going out of the kitchen-door, has turned and tiptoed to the door of the cow-shed; he opens it, and slips inside. Eventually, his curiosity compels him to clamber up to the barred lunette above, where his face becomes visible from time to time.*

THE FARMER: (*showing in* CONSALVO) Come in, sir, come in. What dreadful weather.

CONSALVO: (*peremptorily*) Look, my good man, have you seen a girl anywhere round here? A rather tall, good-looking girl, in a white jacket and a blue dress?

THE FARMER: A girl?

CONSALVO: Yes, yes, a girl. A girl.

THE FARMER: (*laughing for no apparent reason*) A blue dress?

CONSALVO: (*irritated*) Yes, blue, blue. That was what I said. Blue. Francesca, her name was.

THE FARMER: Oh: let's hope it still is, sir. I'll go and

ask the wife. (*He goes over to the other door and asks quickly*) Seen a girl, Mrs.? No? No. (*Turning back*) No, sir, she says she hasn't seen any girl like the one you say, sir.

NOEMI *enters.*

CONSALVO: (*threateningly*) Young man, that girl was seen coming in here.

THE FARMER: (*plaintively*) In here, sir? Why, sir, how can you think . . . why, sir, may I lose my sight and speech if ever I . . .

NOEMI: Well, before that happens, would you be so good as to tell the young lady that her friend Noemi Bata is here, and it's extremely important that I should speak to her . . . that is (*loudly*) unless the young lady has some reason for being ashamed, and feels she ought to hide.

FRANCESCA: (*who has evidently been hiding behind the kitchen door, enters, prepared for battle.*) And why should I be ashamed, or try to hide, may I ask?

The FARMER *withdraws strategically.*

CONSALVO: (*aggressively*) what else are we to expect from behaviour like this, young lady? (*With intense fury*) Young lady: I'd like you to know that I'm a man with a great deal of very important business on my hands; my time is precious. At this moment I ought to be hundreds of miles away from here, sitting at a desk with five telephones on it, and a crowd of extremely important and very touchy business gentlemen waiting to see me. Do you know why I'm here, instead, soaking wet, worn out, and nothing to eat since first thing this morning? (*Breaks off and begins afresh*) Listen: you've read or heard about the famous little mouse, haven't you? The dear little, sweet little, classic little mouse; who gets stuck in the wires at the power-station and puts a whole city out of action? Paralyses trains and factories and central heating and bells and trams all over the whole capital. Well, that's what your friend has done for me. (*Steadily angrier*) One day *he* comes on to the scene: and the staggering capacity he's shown for bringing calamity on everyone from every single thing he does, has something quite fantastic about it. He's run amok over everything, everything we had in the world; like a bull, let loose in a china-shop.

FRANCESCA: A bull, or a mouse, sir?

CONSALVO: The name of the animal is of no moment! My sister and I, in the vortex of disaster that young man has thrown us into, my poor sister and I decided to choose the lesser of two evils in the hope of straightening things out . . .

NOEMI: Consalvo . . .

CONSALVO: This is no time for delicacy, my dear. My sister might have agreed to sacrifice herself, if it were not for what has happened today: your thoughtless and highly significant gesture . . . ah, um, *action*, committed against the person of Mr. Moesse, made it clear that a situation existed of which we were unaware . . . a delicate situation, compelling us to conclude that you yourself entertain a certain interest—that is to say, ah, certain feelings for the . . . the individual aforesaid.

FRANCESCA: (*calmly*) The interest I entertain for the person you . . . refer to above, is one of the most complete indifference. (*A pause.*)

CONSALVO: You speak very definitely on that point. Is that the truth?

FRANCESCA: Of course.

CONSALVO: Ah. I see. (*Gravely*) In that case perhaps I can see about drying my feet. (*He retires to the fireplace, and begins to dry his feet.*)

FRANCESCA: You can keep him, Noemi. He is all yours.

NOEMI: (*innocently*) What on earth are you talking about? Really! Do you think he's . . . amusing? The right sort, would you say?

FRANCESCA: (*spitefully*) My dear, it depends entirely on what you think you can get used to.

NOEMI: (*agreeing*) Oh, yes, of course. No one's going to pretend he's very striking in any way.

FRANCESCA: Good heavens, no. Poor boy, he's terribly country-bred, to put it mildly. He's really only happy when he's gnawing a leg of chicken with his fingers, or sitting about in his shirt-sleeves.

NOEMI: Well, that's not a crime.

FRANCESCA: And physically, of course . . .

NORMI: Oh, I agree, he isn't much to——

FRANCESCA:—not much to write home about, no. And a bit sloppy, of course, most of the time. As for his brain-power . . .

NOEMI: Pretty ordinary that, I'd have said?

FRANCESCA: Almost non-existent. (*In a single breath*) He's suffered from chilblains ever since he was a child; Aunt Ofelia says he snores; Aunt Cleofe calls him a turnip; and he's putting on weight, rather, now . . . though . . . all told, he isn't too bad, I suppose.

NOEMI: All the same, he isn't exactly your ideal, is he?

FRANCESCA: Good heavens, no. God forbid.

The cows have begun to sound rather restless.

NOEMI: Oh, my dear; if you only knew what a weight you'd lifted from my mind.

FRANCESCA: (*suspiciously*) Why?

NOEMI: I was afraid Alberto rather attracted you. I was feeling rather guilty.

FRANCESCA: Guilty? What for?

NOEMI: Well, because, you see . . . *I* like Alberto very much indeed.

FRANCESCA: (*indignantly*) But you just said you thought he was a terribly commonplace young man.

NOEMI: (*triumphantly, and very spitefully*) But that's just the very reason, my dear! All I meant was . . . he's a *good* boy; he'll never be one of those big neurotic types; and he'll make a delightful companion. (*As though revealing a secret*) I've lived a little longer than you, Francesca; and I have to confess that I find Alberto enchanting. He's so stupid. And so sly, and even deceitful, at times . . . and yet, somehow, so sincere, in his own way . . . I dare say the overbearing, worldly, cynical type of man may seem very attractive to a country girl; but I'm a woman. And in any case there must be a certain amount of honey in Alberto; or there wouldn't be so many flies buzzing round him. His wife will have to be very careful. (*A tiny pause.*) And I . . . *shall* be careful, my dear. (*A pause.*)

FRANCESCA: (*angrily*) You mean you're going to marry him?

NOEMI: Well, what do you think? I adore him.

FRANCESCA: (*very spitefully*) Well, at your time of life, I suppose it's understandable. When there's no roast beef available, we have to make do with a turnip.

NOEMI: (*not pleased*) Francesca; while we're on the

subject: weren't *you* in love with Alberto once upon a time?

FRANCESCA: With Alberto? *Me?*

NOEMI: Yes. Don't you remember the things you used to say about him at school? You said you'd die, without Alberto? M'm? Didn't you?

FRANCESCA: My dear, I was a little girl then. I didn't know him properly in those days.

NOEMI: Do you think you know him properly now? My poor dear Francesca; it's not the same man. The boy who whispers sweet nothings into the ears of schoolgirls isn't the same person as the man who has breathed the fragrance of a full-grown woman. No, you don't know Alberto! He can be jealous; did you know that? He can be a bit of a tyrant, a bully . . . Because you see, dear: he loves me. That's what it is. He loves me.

FRANCESCA: (*who has been much pained by these words*) I don't believe it. It's a pack of lies.

NOEMI: I wouldn't like you to suffer from a broken heart. He loves me.

FRANCESCA: Alberto isn't that sort.

NOEMI: No, I know: you think he's a turnip. A young man can always be a turnip when he wants to.

FRANCESCA: (*furiously*) What do you mean?

NOEMI: When a woman means nothing to him. And suffers. It must make him laugh, rather, don't you think?

FRANCESCA: I don't know what you mean!

NOEMI: But it's written all over your face, dear! I can just see the two of you: you, pestering him with little presents and cakes and woollies: and Alberto as cold as an icicle. You shouldn't have been so pressing, perhaps, dear; you ought to have held off a bit more. Still, what can one do when one's in love? One can suffer horribly, I know. I understand just how you feel. And then, after all that! To see him married to someone else!

A long pause.

FRANCESCA: (*stands there breathing hard for a moment, uncertain whether to burst into tears or to seize* NOEMI *by the hair; suddenly it flashes on her that there is another way of discomfiting her adversary, and she becomes calm again.*) Well, if you really have seen all that's been going on, I suppose it's useless for me to try and keep my secret any longer.

NOEMI: What do you mean?

FRANCESCA: Well, just *that*, Alberto did see that I was in love with him.

NOEMI: Well?

ALBERTO'S *face appears at the grille.*

FRANCESCA: He . . . took advantage of the fact.

NOEMI: What?

FRANCESCA: He took advantage.

Pause. Then an intensified, disturbed mooing is heard from the stable. ALBERTO'S *face has vanished.*

CONSALVO: (*violently to* NOEMI) I said it! Didn't I! I said it myself. I said I didn't like the young man! You've always had a weakness for these Bohemian types, Noemi.

NOEMI: And do you really think I'm going to believe a piece of nonsense like that, Francesca?

FRANCESCA: You don't believe it?

NOEMI: Of course I don't. I'm not a fool.

FRANCESCA: You don't believe that Alberto and I . . .

NOEMI: It's a stupid lie.

FRANCESCA: (*determined by now to invent any absurdity in order to defeat her rival*) Very well, since you insist, I shall have to tell you everything; though God knows I've never wanted to tell anyone. These . . . things . . . as we all know . . . often have their Fatal Consequences. So did this. Yes. (*She delicately indicates the length of a rather well-grown baby*).

CONSALVO: (*pushing his hands through his hair*) My God!

There are renewed bellowings from the cows.

FRANCESCA: That puts a stop to your little schemes, doesn't it, Noemi?

NOEMI: It's a silly, outrageous, childish lie. You make me laugh. You're just making it up to try and make things difficult between me and Alberto.

FRANCESCA: I am a victim, and I have my rights.

NOEMI: It's not true, it's not true!

FRANCESCA: We shall see.

NOEMI: We'll ask Alberto.

FRANCESCA: Ask him by all means.

CONSALVO: (*wandering up and down, his hands in his hair*) My God, what a hell of a mess!

THE FARMER: (*appearing for a moment at the door as the cows bellow still louder*) Please, please, ladies and gentlemen, you're frightening my poor cows. It'll turn their milk. (*He retires.*)

NOEMI: (*to* FRANCESCA) You're a little liar!

FRANCESCA: He seduced me. He knows where his duty lies.

NOEMI: It's not true. Alberto loves me. Al . . .

FRANCESCA: Alberto.

CONSALVO: Alberto! Alberto! What in God's name ever brought him across my path?

The noise has risen to a climax. Suddenly they all turn to the door, as AUNT CLEOFE *enters, shutting a groaning umbrella.*

CLEOFE: May I ask . . . Oh, Francesca, thank goodness you're here. May I ask what that fool of a boy is up to?

CONSALVO: Of whom are you speaking, madam?

CLEOFE: Why, Alberto, of course.

CONSALVO: And why have you come to look for him here?

CLEOFE: Don't be ridiculous. He came in here. He told us to wait for him a moment down at the crossroads. We've been waiting there half an hour in the pouring rain.

CONSALVO *has understood. His eyes turn to the cow-shed door. A tense pause. The mooing has ceased; suddenly, the tiny wail of a new-born calf is heard.* CONSALVO *marches determinedly to the door of the shed and throws it open.* ALBERTO *is still clinging to the bars of the grille. His feet are not touching the ground.*

CONSALVO: Come down, Mr. Moesse. And stop molesting those unfortunate animals.

ALBERTO: (*stiffly*) I . . . I couldn't find my hat. (*He comes into the room; a certain amount of straw clings to him.*)

CONSALVO: (*cold and angry*) Never mind about your hat, for the moment; leave it. I wish to speak to you.

(*Dropping his voice a little*) Now, sir; what is this extraordinary tale we hear? Is it true that you have misbehaved yourself with this young lady.

ALBERTO *turns to* FRANCESCA, *and gives her a look of understanding; then he answers* CONSALVO.

ALBERTO: (*martyred and stoical*) I cannot deny it, sir.

CONSALVO: (*sceptically*) And is it true that there have been . . . um, ah . . . Fatal Consequences?

ALBERTO: (*even more stoically*) I cannot deny it, sir. I know where my duty lies.

CONSALVO: (*fiercely*) Then it's quite clear you and your friend must think I look like an imbecile.

ALBERTO: (*lost in thought*) I cannot deny it, sir.

CONSALVO: You listen to me. I did first of all think, since you are now an employee of my bank, of sending you to our branch in Madagascar.

ALBERTO: Madagascar, sir? Why?

CONSALVO: Yellow fever is said to be raging there. I had hoped you might catch it. But I realised on reflection that your mere decease would solve nothing. Whatever may be the purpose of the infantile lies invented by that young woman and confirmed by yourself, the one clear fact is that you have publicly disgraced the good name of my sister and myself. I consider it essential on behalf of my sister and myself that you should repair the damage you have done. And repair it you shall! Mr. Moesse, you will kindly demand of me in the warmest manner you can command, the hand of my sister in . . .

NOEMI: (*low*) No, Consalvo. I've given him up.

CONSALVO: What? What do you mean?

NOEMI: I want no more to do with him.

CONSALVO: (*outraged*) You mean you're throwing the whole thing up?

NOEMI: Yes.

CONSALVO: (*aghast, and trying to coax her*) But, Noemi, my dear: you've been hammering it into my head for days; you've compelled me to fabricate things which might have come from some cheap novelette; you've made me traipse hundreds of miles under blazing sun and pouring rain. And after all that, you say you're going to give him up. All this tarradiddle about duty and fatal consequences and I don't know what, is just a tale they've made up to deceive us: surely you must see that? This young man has simply told a lie!

NOEMI: (*low*) It was his telling the lie that made me realise . . . that I've never meant anything to him. (*She weeps.*)

FRANCESCA: (*suddenly*) Ah, no! Don't cry, Noemi! Don't cry, my dear, don't cry. (*Goes across to* NOEMI, *who puts her head on* FRANCESCA'S *shoulder, and continues to weep;* FRANCESCA *gently strokes her.*)

CONSALVO: Come, come, Noemi.

NOEMI: I want to go away . . . Take me away.

CONSALVO: Of course, my dear.

NOEMI: I want to go home.

CONSALVO: Yes, my dear. We'll go. We'll go back home. Come.

FRANCESCA: Don't cry, Noemi. He isn't worth it. No man's worth a woman crying over him.

Supported by FRANCESCA, NOEMI, *still in tears, goes to the door. The unfortunate* ALBERTO *is standing apart in disgrace.*

ALBERTO: (*stepping forward, stammering*) I . . . I only wanted to say that . . . in view of the . . . the disclosure, I mean . . . I am prepared to . . . marry her.

CLEOFE: (*like a pistol-shot*) Which!

ALBERTO (*frightened*) Why . . . F-Francesca.

FRANCESCA: (*scornfully*) Disclosure! (*Solemnly*) Allow me to tell *you*, Alberto Moesse, that I wouldn't marry you, now, not even if they fetched the police and ordered me to. Come, Noemi, darling, let's leave him.

There is a pause as they go out, leaving ALBERTO *and* CLEOFE *behind. The outer door is heard opening and closing.*

ALBERTO: (*indignantly*) I see. Did you hear that, Aunt Cleofe? Fine, isn't it? I give up a splendid career and a magnificent marriage. I run the risk of being sent to Madagascar and dying of yellow fever. I'm pushed over a cliff, I get soaked to the skin, I'm forced to hide in a stable, I allow myself to be described as a vile seducer: I, who could be pointed to as an example of virtue and chastity; and after all that . . . I find a girl saying to me . . . what did she say?

CLEOFE: That she wouldn't marry you even if they fetched the police.

ALBERTO: Grateful, isn't it? Just so as not to contradict her: out of sheer delicacy, I let people believe I'm not only a seducer, and an illegitimate father, I let people defame me, slander me . . . and then . . . then . . . But do you know what I shall do? I'll marry the other! I'll marry Noemi. I'll just go and find my hat, and then I'll . . . (*He breaks off.*)

FRANCESCA: (*entering hastily*) Noemi left her scarf and

mackintosh. Where . . . ? Oh, thank you, Aunt Cleofe, I'll be back in a . . .

ALBERTO: (*at once timid and brusque*) Francesca: you . . . you said you wouldn't marry me not even . . .

FRANCESCA: Not even if they fetched the police.

ALBERTO: I see; good. After all I've done for you. I'm glad to hear it. I know now what I must do, do you see? It wasn't because I was fond of you, see? I did it . . . just to help you, to make you happy. (*Wildly*) Were you, or were you not, in love with me?

FRANCESCA: I was, my dear. And now . . . a miracle's happened, Aunt Cleofe! I'm not, any longer. Do you know, all at once I realised, suddenly. It's all over. Like that. As if my sight had suddenly been restored.

ALBERTO: Your what?

FRANCESCA: (*aggressively*) My sight. Restored. I can see you now as you are. And I don't want you any more.

CLEOFE: (*vibrantly*) Good, Francesca. Splendid. You can always find people like him. You're cleverer than he is, and yet you loved him. He'd have made a victim of you.

FRANCESCA: I'm not such a fool as that.

CONSALVO: (*off*) Miss Francesca!

FRANCESCA: I'm just coming! . . . I really feel quite astounded to think I ever saw anything in him.

CLEOFE: (*briskly*) Francesca: the doctor is waiting just down the road. In these things it's always best to follow one's instincts and strike while the iron is hot. Do you want me to tell him to come up here?

FRANCESCA: Yes, Aunt. Yes. Certainly.

CONSALVO: (*off*) Miss Francesca!

FRANCESCA: (*giving* NOEMI'S *things to* CLEOFE) Will you please give them these things, Aunt Cleofe, and say goodbye to them for me? And tell the doctor to come in here.

CLEOFE: Yes, my dear, of course. I will.

CLEOFE *withdraws.*

ALBERTO: (*angrily*) What utter nonsense! I suppose you think you can make me angry? Some hopes. How stupid. Sight restored, indeed. I never heard such nonsense.

FRANCESCA: Yes, Alberto. You went on too long, seeing nothing.

ALBERTO: Yes, because I've no brains, because I'm backward!

FRANCESCA: No: I was used to that. I'd accepted it. It was when you admitted you'd had your way with me ... with "fatal consequences". You poor creature.

ALBERTO: (*furious*) But I only said that so that they wouldn't find you out in a lie! Did you say it, or didn't you?

FRANCESCA: Yes, but you let them believe it! You were delighted. You went too far.

ALBERTO: *Me!*

FRANCESCA: Yes. And I suddenly felt such contempt for you, such loathing ...

ALBERTO: Oh! So you loathe me now, do you? Let me tell you ...

FRANCESCA: Alberto: when I look back on all the things I've done for you, all these years, but especially today, I shudder at the thought of it. Good evening, Doctor.

The DOCTOR *has entered.*

THE DOCTOR: (*who has evidently prepared a difficult speech which he is bent on delivering*) Good evening. Your respected aunt, who has for many years now honoured me . . .

ALBERTO: (*sweeping him aside*) The things you've done for me? What do you . . . ?

FRANCESCA: Yes, it was all your fault. You roused awful criminal instincts in me, from deep down.

ALBERTO: Doctor: I'm a criminal influence now!

THE DOCTOR: Your respected aunt, whose continued confidence in me . . .

FRANCESCA: (*ignoring him*) Yes, all those lies and impostures: they were all your fault!

THE DOCTOR: Your respected aunt . . .

FRANCESCA: You forced me to make up the most disgusting tales, and deceive decent and well-meaning people; you made me push you off the mountain!

ALBERTO: (*ferociously*) And I suppose all these scratches on my face are my fault, eh?

FRANCESCA: Yes. And you made me make up nasty immoral stories and be a laughing-stock to everyone, as if I were another Noemi, half-dressed in a hut for cement and hydraulic lime!

ALBERTO: Doctor, she says it was me!

THE DOCTOR: The reason I am persuaded to present myself here . . .

ALBERTO (*brushing him away*) It's my fault if it rains, I suppose? If the cows' milk goes wrong tomorrow, it's all because of me!

FRANCESCA: Of course it is. You made me ashamed of myself. And now it's over, you understand? Even if I did once feel a little fond of you, it's all over and done with now. Ah, Doctor, if you only know how happy I feel! Let's go, Doctor, I seem to be breathing fresh air for the first time for years.

THE DOCTOR: The true reason for my visit here . . .

ALBERTO: (*shouts*) All right then, if you want to know, I used to be in love with *you*! Once. I never realised: but whenever I used to come back home, in the train, I was as happy as anything; I used to whistle so loudly that everyone used to turn round and look. (A man once told me to stop. "Stop it," he said.) And do you know why I was happy? It was because of you. Because I was going to see you so soon, and talk to you. A little while ago, when I came down the mountain to look for you, I got soaked to the skin, I might have fallen in a ditch; and died, too. And I would never have complained. Why? Because it was all for you! I might have caught a chill—and perhaps I have caught one, too: listen: (*He forces a cough.*) And it didn't matter, because I loved you. And *now*, do you want to know? Exactly the same thing has happened to me. It's all over.

FRANCESCA: It is just as well.

ALBERTO: In the very moment when I realised that I'd always loved you, ever since I was a boy, in that very same moment, *bonk*! It was all over.

THE DOCTOR: It is precisely for that reason, Miss Francesca, that your aunt, who . . .

ALBERTO: (*shouting*) You've told too many lies! I can't bear people who tell lies. This is the end. It's all over. And better for everyone.

FRANCESCA: Certainly it's better for everyone. Goodnight. Doctor, you were quite right to come.

ALBERTO: (*beside himself*) I'll marry Noemi. I've made up my mind. I'll go and get my hat, and then I'll marry her. She really loves me. (*He goes out to the cowshed.*)

THE DOCTOR: Miss Francesca: your respected aunt, who has for many years honoured me with her trust, has been so kind as to advise me that I now might, or rather must, or (to put it more accurately perhaps) that the moment has now arrived when ...

ALBERTO: (*reappearing, furious*) Look at it! Look at my hat! The cows have been trampling all over it. Even my hat's ruined! Never mind, though!

FRANCESCA: It's useless running after Noemi. She has already told you ...

ALBERTO: (*disgusted*) That she won't have me either, yes! First you all want me, then none of you want me. The sincerity of it! Never mind, I'll go my own way, I don't care a damn for any of you! Do you see what the result is? I've caught a cold. (*He makes himself cough.*) I knew it. I can feel a tickling in my throat, it's always the sign. Goodbye.

FRANCESCA: Goodbye.

ALBERTO: (*furiously*) And if you want to know, I don't want either of you: neither you nor her! You don't deserve me! You don't understand me! Even with you, I should always have been wasted. You're just a little hypocrite, that's all. A little snake in the grass.

FRANCESCA: And you're a liar!

ALBERTO: (*shouts*) I like sincere, genuine people who say what they mean! An old cabbage like the doctor, that's the sort of thing you deserve.

THE DOCTOR: Oh, please, I beg you ...

FRANCESCA: You don't even make me angry; I just feel sorry for you.

THE DOCTOR: And I never touch cabbage, as it happens.

FRANCESCA: What do you expect of him, Doctor: he's just a bad lot.

THE DOCTOR: (*scientifically*) Psychologically a sub-normal—the debile-unstable type . . .

ALBERTO: What?

THE DOCTOR: . . . with characteristics of turbulent immorality and antisocial egotism. The two often go together.

ALBERTO: (*taking a large brush from the hearth and brandishing it*) Doctor: would you be so good as to explain what you think you're doing here?

THE DOCTOR: The young lady's aunt, whose complete trust in me sometimes surprises me . . .

ALBERTO: There's nothing for you to do here! There's no one ill here.

THE DOCTOR: (*bitingly*) Who knows, who can tell? A good doctor is always useful.

ALBERTO: But if anything were to happen to *you* in here, we should need another doctor.

THE DOCTOR: Please, please. Come. Come-come-come. I am here in order to offer this young lady the disinterested support of a gentleman . . . who is, I may say, (*with a contemptuous glance at* ALBERTO) a real man, who has his head fixed on in the correct manner, the right way round!

ALBERTO: Oh, you have, have you? Just explain what you mean by that.

THE DOCTOR: (*solemnly, with a pitying look at* ALBERTO)

I am here, Miss Francesca, to place my mackintosh round your shoulders, so that you do not get wet as you issue from these premises, and so that you may, also, from that simple gesture, divine what it means to have ever at your side a person . . . whom not even the rain can take by surprise.

ALBERTO: But she can have *my* mackintosh!

FRANCESCA: (*dignified*) No, Alberto. It is too late.

THE DOCTOR: You, sir, have already demonstrated your unsuitability. Allow me . . . (*He puts his mackintosh round* FRANCESCA'S *shoulders.*)

FRANCESCA: Thank you, Doctor. (*Pause: then, sadly*) Alberto: there comes a day in our lives when we wake up in the morning still a child . . . and by nightfall we have become grown-up. The time for games and day-dreaming is over.

THE DOCTOR: And more durative affections supervene, calculated to be a stay and comfort in the inevitable rubs and misfortunes of later life.

FRANCESCA: (*tears in her voice*) Goodbye, Alberto. It used to be so lovely to hear your voice in the garden . . .

ALBERTO: (*huskily*) Do you remember, Francesca . . . those picnics together: such splendid jam. What appetites we had, how happy we were . . .

FRANCESCA: (*much moved*) And now the garden will never again seem to me so beautiful or so green, the days will never again have such a bloom upon them . . .

ALBERTO: (*almost crying*) What makes me sorrier than anything, oh my poor Francesca, is the thought of leaving you there (*with sincere desolation*) in the hands of that dreadful old quack . . .

FRANCESCA: (*with melancholy resignation*) How should it be else, Alberto?

THE DOCTOR: I must say I find that remark rather questionably put!

ALBERTO: A man who will always rouse shivers of disgust in you . . .

THE DOCTOR: I would ask you kindly to note . . .

FRANCESCA: I shall try my best, Alberto.

ALBERTO: You will pass your days surrounded by the stink of carbolic acid and mortuary chambers . . . And my own life . . . will be no better. (*Moving away, almost weeping*) Goodbye, Francesca.

FRANCESCA: (*stopping him, tremulously*) Alberto. Where are you going now?

ALBERTO: (*tragically*) Where should I go? I don't know.

FRANCESCA: Don't be silly. You can't go out like that without your hat. You're still soaking wet.

ALBERTO: (*with melancholy indifference*) What should it matter to me any more?

The FARMER *has just entered, carrying a tray.*

FARMER: Young sir: here's your coffee: you're not going away without drinking it, are you?

ALBERTO: (*staggered*) *My* coffee?

FRANCESCA: (*dropping her eyes*) Yes. I asked them to make some for you, Alberto. I saw how wet you were, and . . . (*Suddenly energetic, she pushes him towards the fire.*) Can't you ever realise how delicate you are? You must look after yourself, or you really will catch cold, of course you will. Come here, come and drink this nice coffee; sit down there, near the fire. The coffee will do you good.

ALBERTO: (*sits*) Oh, how *kind* you are, Francesca! (*He begins to stir his coffee, looking triumphantly at the* DOCTOR.)

FRANCESCA: (*with dignity, removing the mackintosh from her shoulders, and restoring it to the* DOCTOR) I must return your mackintosh to you, Doctor. Thank you. You are able to think of such things for yourself. But Alberto isn't. He has to have someone to think of them for him.

THE DOCTOR: But what of his outrageous conduct? What of that?

FRANCESCA: This is the only way I know to make him pay for it. (*She points to* ALBERTO, *who coughs.*) Doctor, is that cough serious do you think?

THE DOCTOR: As a general rule, such coughs are of but little moment. Nonetheless and unfortunately, one can occasionally begin by having a slight cough . . . and that slight cough can quickly lead to the grave. (*Courteously, raising his hat*) And should that happen in this case, Miss Francesca, if you would like me to . . . then I will, all patiently, *wait.*

ALBERTO *bends down impetuously and picks up the fire-tongs from the hearth. The* DOCTOR, *putting the worst construction on this gesture, disappears rapidly.*

THE END